Mirfield

Landscape and People to 1500 AD

Joan Thornes and Hilary Brook

Ash Tree Publications

2016

ISBN 978-0-9517222-8-2

Designed by Robin Thornes
Typset in Minion Pro

Published by Ash Tree Publications

Printed by Amadeus Press, Ezra House, Littlewood Drive
Cleckheaton, West Yorkshire, BD19 4TQ

Contents

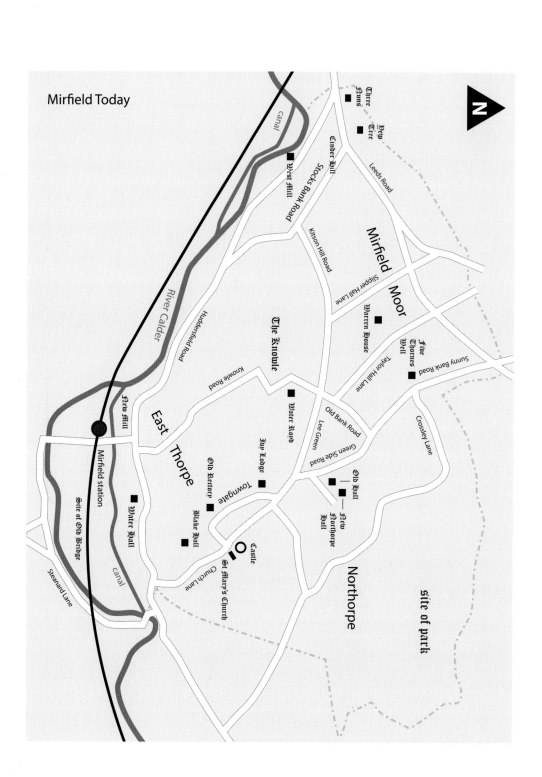

Mirfield Today

N

Canal

Three
Nuns

Yew
Tree

Leeds Road

West Mill

Cimber Hill

Stocks Bank Road

Mirfield

Kitson Hill Road

Slipper Hall Lane

Moor

Warren House

River Calder

The Knowle

Five
Thornes
Well

Taylor Hall Lane

Sunny Bank Road

Huddersfield Road

Knowle Road

Water Royd

Old Bank Road

Crossley Lane

Green Side Road

Lee Green

New Mill

East
Thorpe

Ivy Lodge

Old Rectory

Towngate

Old Hall

New
Northorpe
Hall

Mirfield station

Site of Old Bridge

Water Hall

Blake Hall

Castle

St Mary's Church

Church Lane

Northorpe

site of park

Steanard Lane

Canal

Introduction

The first map of Mirfield township was made in 1819 by Henry Harling, a land surveyor who lived in the nearby village of Hopton. On it were drawn the boundaries of the recently enclosed parcels of land that had been allocated to those freeholders who had been awarded a share of the previously open commons. More than twenty years had elapsed since an Act of Parliament in 1798 allowed the enclosure of the commons and waste and the remnant of the medieval common fields of Mirfield. A large part of the landscape had been changed within a few years. The 438 acre expanse of Mirfield Moor had become a patchwork of small fields and all the other small pieces of common land, more than another 50 acres were also now enclosed. This redistribution of land was one of the biggest and most rapidly executed changes to a landscape where for centuries change had been piecemeal and usually slow. Harling's map also showed boundaries that had been there for centuries and revealed the pattern of the medieval landscape of Mirfield. Despite the many changes since 1819 many of these old boundaries are still in place today, preserved as boundaries of more recent developments and influencing the layout of roads and streets.

Since that first map was drawn in 1819 much has changed. Mirfield is no longer a place of open landscape dotted with farms and small hamlets, Towngate, Northorpe, Earthorpe (now Easthorpe) and that near the Nunbrook at the western end of the township. By the beginning of the twentieth century it had become a busy and thriving town, an urban district council of the West Riding with a district council and a town hall. New turnpike roads, a canal, railways, coal mining, the woollen industry, malting and boat building had all contributed to a century of growth and development. In 1822 Edward Baines *Directory of the West Riding* informed its readers:

> Mirfield is now principally distinguished as one of the favourite seats of the woollen manufacture, and as a centre of this staple trade' It is a fertile, opulent and delightfully situated village, and from its ancient history, and present respectability, is well entitled to a somewhat elaborate notice.

Thirty or so years later White's *Directory of the Clothing Districts of the West Riding* in 1851 described Mirfield as 'a scattered but populous, clothing village bearing different names, and stretching a considerable distance along the north bank of the Calder'. By 1861 the *Post Office Directory* felt it correct to describe Mirfield as a 'town' which *Slater's Directory* of 1891 described as 'situated in a pleasant, fertile neighbourhood amidst delightful scenery'.

The Rev H. N. Pobjoy was to write of Mirfield 'as it was in the earlier part of the twentieth century before modern housing developments had altered its appearance, and obliterated many open spaces, and before many old buildings had been demolished'. The changes have continued and the town he remembered 'as it was until the 1920s is no longer recognizable. More of the older houses, mills and other industrial buildings have gone, and railways have been dismantled, the cuttings and embankments levelled and the older hamlets are part of the modern agglomeration of housing.

This new look at the history of Mirfield is the story of a changing landscape and of the people who have lived here. It begins when the last Ice Age had ended, roughly 11,500 years ago, and finishes at the end of the medieval period. An end date of 1500 AD has been chosen, although no period of history has an abrupt end. From the surviving fragments of documentary evidence, plans and maps, especially that made by Henry Harling, and field work, it has been possible to reconstruct much of the pattern of the medieval landscape in Mirfield and say something of the people. There is no such evidence for these things for prehistoric or Roman times, and the story for those times can only be reconstructed using any slight evidence and the archaeological evidence available for the wider region of south-west Yorkshire.

The scope of this book is restricted to that of the Domesday Book vill or township of Mirfield, which included what is now Ravensthorpe, but not Hopton. The River Calder is the natural boundary between Mirfield and Hopton and Domesday Book in 1086 records them as two separate vills which by then were included in the feudal barony known as the Honour of Pontefract, lands belonging to the Norman, Ilbert de Lacy. The history and development of Hopton is a story for which the information is very scanty until the records of the civil parish of Mirfield, which included Hopton, begin in the seventeenth century. Then the parish was the unit of local administration responsible for the maintenance of the highways, of law and order and the relief of the poor and Hopton appears more frequently in the record.

Historically, a separate manor of Hopton seems to have survived through the centuries. It was mentioned in Domesday book but references to this manor only appears again in the sixteenth century. There seems to have been one small manorial hamlet adjacent to Hopton Hall. Other settlement has been as scattered farmsteads of which nothing is known in medieval sources.

The need for a history of Mirfield which would include that of the landscape seemed important as houses might be built on fields that still preserved features of the medieval landscape. The features of some of Mirfield's medieval common fields are still to be seen and have been described by Hilary, whose special interest and knowledge of them is well illustrated here. Some of the evidence relating to the medieval landscape and settlements has raised problems, one being the identification of the original Northorpe Hall. These difficulties have been much discussed and then resolved to our mutual satisfaction. For trying to place the the information in its wider environmental, archaeological and historical context and for any errors so made I take full responsibility. Our conclusions are a "best fit' using the evidence available.

Finally, acknowledgement must be made for help given by the archivists at West Yorkshire Archive Sevices at Wakefield, Calderdale (Halifax), Kirklees (Huddersfield), Nottingham County Records Office and Yorkshire Archaeological Society. To Peter Thornes and Malcolm Brook for flying over the area looking for crop marks and taking photographs and Chris and Janice Barker for permission to use photographs taken by A.H. Barker. Lastly, Robin Thornes of Ash Tree Publications is to be thanked for the invaluable work of preparing the maps and text for publication.

Notes for the Reader

As this is intended for the general reader the text has not been loaded with footnotes and references, but quotations have been referenced or acknowledged. Any dates mentioned are given, where necessary, in the traditional style as BC (Before Christ), and AD (Anno Domini). The word medieval has been preferred to the alternative 'middle ages', and in this account applies to the time between Domesday Book and around 1500 AD.

Joan Thornes 2016

CHAPTER ONE

Mirfield Township

At some unknown time, possibly in the eighth or ninth century, and well before Mirfield appears in Domesday Book, the boundaries that marked out the medieval township had been fixed. Within them was an area of approximately two thousand acres of land, high ground, middle slopes and some on the river flood plain, sufficient land to support the settlement to which it was attached and whose inhabitants would have a common responsibility for any payment demanded by an overlord or the king. The eastern boundary was fixed on the small river now known as the Spen, but whose old name was the Ravensbrook, the name which will occasionally be used here. The River Calder provided the boundary on the south side and another rivulet, later known as the Nunbrook, that on the west. There was less clear definition on the north side, across the high ground, where a small watercourse in the north-west side and another on the north-east, now the Finching Dike, left a gap to be marked between them; in later times this was to be a wall. To the north were the lands that became the territories of Hartshead and Liversedge. These ancient boundaries are still observed today with the exception of the more recent one between Dewsbury (Ravensthorpe) and Mirfield across the south-east corner. It was here that there was rapid change in the nineteenth century. By the mid century, as industrial development and housing spread over the arable fields and riverside meadows, this area was known as Newtown, but later re-named Ravensthorpe. This part of Mirfield township was incorporated into Dewsbury Borough in 1911.

The Topography – the shape of the land

The greater part of Mirfield lies on a broad, south facing spur of land situated on the north side of the River Calder. The highest and most exposed area, Mirfield Moor, is near the northern boundary where, from OD 130m (425 feet) near the Warren House, the land falls away to OD 45m (150ft) on the floodplain of the Calder. The steepest slopes of the spur are on the south-western side, with the most severe being between Quarry Bank, Battyeford. and Stocksbank. Here the steep, rocky outcrop has

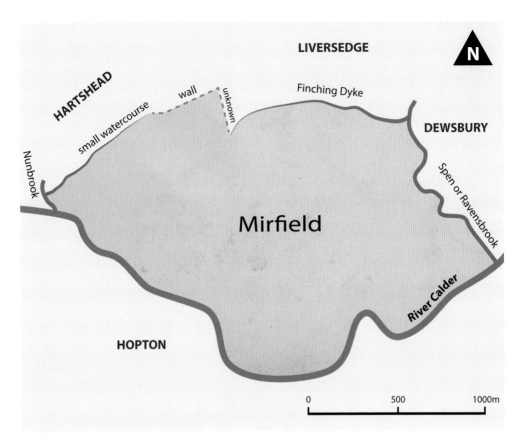

The boundaries of the township.

been extensively quarried in the past. The more gradual slopes are south and eastwards to Easthorpe and then by a sharp dip to the flood plain, a broad semi circular level extending southwards to the river. On the eastern side the spur has a well defined edge, a shallow sandstone escarpment which runs southward from its high point at Crossley Hill, OD 127 m (415 ft) to Shillbank. From the foot of this escarpment the land slopes gradually towards the east to the levels between the Spen and the Calder. The narrow ridge on which St. Mary's church stands is separated from the main body of the spur by a valley which follows the line of slipping of the underlying rocks.

The Geology

The underlying rocks which give shape to the landscape are those typical of the Middle Coal Measures of south-west Yorkshire. As the name implies, coal is a characteristic mineral of this geology. It is found between layers of sedimentary rocks, the sandstones, mudstones or shales and clays. All these mineral have been valuable resources in the past, coal, rubble stone and building stone and the material for brick making, although none of them are extracted at the present day. The hard rocks, the sandstones, are of two very similar types and have been used as building stone in the township. The beds of Clifton and Fallhouse rock; are so named because of their respective positions as layers in the geological sequence; the Fallhouse lies above the Clifton rock. The Falhouse rock forms the long spine of higher ground that runs southward from Crossley Hill and also underlies the Westfield area and the Nab. The Clifton rock, which is lower in the geological sequence, only appears as a narrow band in the southwest part of the township where it outcrops as the long, steep scarp of Quarry Bank. Lying between and above these sandstones are the layers of mudstone, shale, coal and clay, the clays forming the sub surface geology in some areas. Where the clays and shaley rocks have been eroded the sandstones are left as the sub surface geology in other areas. The clayey-shaley strata and coal seams lie above the sandstone over a large area in the northwest part of the township, from the Nab, the Knowle and beyond the Westfield to the northern boundary.

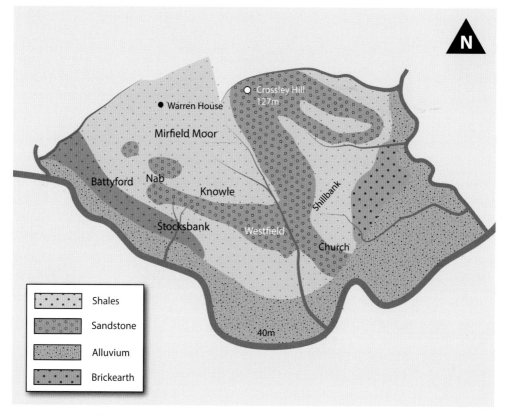

The geology of the Mirfield area.

Coal has been mined since medieval times when there are references from the mid-fourteenth century of men searching and digging for coal (Manor Court Roll). At first the diggings were small scale in places where coal outcropped on the hillsides or could be found not far below the ground surface but by the eighteenth century deeper pits were sunk to reach the more the productive seams. One seam on Mirfield Moor, the 'Blocking Coal' found at a depth of approximately 13m (42 ft), was being mined in the late-eighteenth century and mining continued there until more recent times at Mirfield Moor Colliery. As a result of slipping or faulting in.the underlying rock, the same coal seam occurs at a greater depth further east at Northorpe where it was found at a depth of 38m(125ft) and was worked at Nevin's Colliery, Northorpe, from the late-nineteenth century until 1931.

The Alluvium - gravel and sandy silt

The alluvium that covers the underlying rock strata to form the floodplain of the Calder and the lower reaches of the Spen is, in geological terms, the most recent. These huge quantities of water borne rock fragments, pebbles, clay and sand were deposited here during the last Ice Age when torrents of fast flowing meltwater from the the ice sheets which lay to the north and west poured through the valleys of the Calder and the Spen. As the water slowed in its flow thick layers of the pebbly gravel gradually accumulated, some of which have been identified as pieces of Buttermere and Eskdale granite originating in the Cumbrian fells. These deposits of gravel are often of considerable thickness and in Mirfield vary, 5.5 metres (18 feet) were recorded in borings at Nevin's (Dark Lane) Colliery, Northorpe, and 12 metres (40 feet). at Red Laithes (Ravensthorpe). At Battyeford 9 metres (30 feet) of alluvium was found when excavating for the foundations of Battyeford Bridge. There it fills a deep gorge cut down through the underlying rock by the action of great volumes of water. A narrow and elongated band of brick earth, clay with pockets of gravel, which stretches along the foot of the the high ground below Shillbank and Northorpe may be a remnant of an material deposited during an even earlier Ice Age.

The most recent deposits on the floodplain are the sands and silty soil deposited by flood water and, in some places, by the normal flow of the river. It is the deposition of silt at some points on the river channel and the gradual erosion of the banks in other places that has contributed to changes in the course of the Calder over time. One change has been identified by the presence of a narrow, curved piece of land below Easthorpe that is shown on Harling's map. That has been identified as the 'Dead Eye', a name often given in the past to an old, abandoned loop in the course of a river, something that resulted when a new and straighter channel established itself. The location of

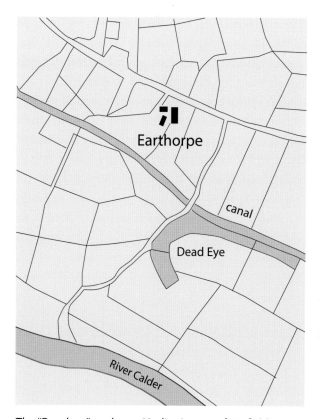

the Dead Eye suggests that the Ea(r)Thorpe (now Easthorpe), 'ea' being old English meaning water and 'thorpe' or hamlet, was nearer the river than it is today. Water Hall was also known as the Earthorpe. It is interesting to note that the present canal probably follows an old course of the river for part of its length. The deposition and washing away of the river bank also resulted in the relocation of the old Mirfield Bridge, later known as Shepley Bridge, downriver to its present position.

The "Deadeye" as shown Harling's map of Mirfield.

Springs and Watercourses

The underground water that emerged as many small springs, or wells as they were called, and the streams, provided all of the water used by the inhabitants. These were features of the historic landscape. The Town Well at the northern end of Towngate like the others had a stone lined depression to collect the water. The natural drainage of the land taking all the surplus water was by the many small watercourses that fed into the main rivulets or streams that flowed south and east into the Calder and the Spen (the Spen then feeding into the Calder). Now much of this water is taken by the modern underground drainage system.

The most important north to south drainage was, and still is, provided by the Town Brook, the name for that stretch of the watercourse alongside which the medieval hamlet of Mirfield Town was situated. Many small streams contributed to the Town Brook, whose source was the Five Thornes Well. Once a public watering place on the part of Mirfield Moor, it was later enclosed by the Taylor Hall brickworks. The name

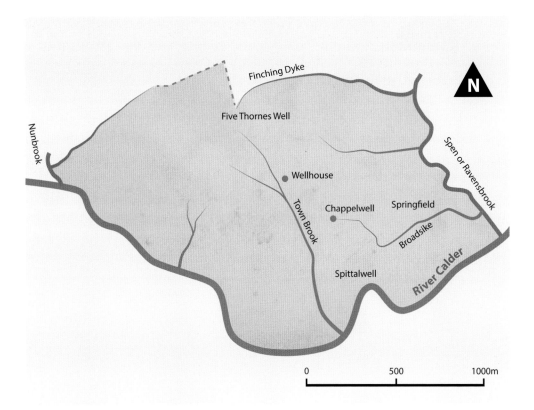

The streams and rivers of the Mirfield area.

Town Brook has disappeared like the water that is now mostly taken underground, although it still emerges into the open at the southern end of Pinfold Lane. From there it remains open for a short length alongside the Blake Hall estate before continuing underground to the river.

The main drainage channel in the eastern part of the township was the Broadsike, later known as Canker Dike. Neither name is applicable now, as the water is also mostly underground. The old name Broadsike translates as 'broad, shallow valley' an unusual feature in an otherwise flat landscape. This shallow valley with its sluggish watercourse may have been, as the topography suggests, a very ancient channel of the river before it moved south to its present course. It took water from the hillside springs and field ditches to the north and west through the low lying land to empty into the Ravensbrook (Spen). The spring at the head of the Broadsike can still be seen in the valley to the north-east of Mirfield church, although the water seems to have once emerged further to the north as Chappel Well on Shillbank. The building of the railway along Shillbank presumably led to the water being taken in an underground drainage pipe to where it can be seen now. Other springs that fed water into the Broadsike were the Spitalwell to the south of Mirfield Church and the springs issuing at Springfield in Northope.

In previous times ditches made to drain water from the fields and the sides of the lanes were of great importance and had to be kept open and free flowing. The importance attached to this is apparent from frequent orders made in the manor court for this work to be done. At one court in 1608 complaint was made that 'William Beaumont did not keep the Spitalwell spring in the watercourse in which it ought to run from the spring to the Broadsike'. In 1613 it was ordered that 'Master William Beaumont shall not release the water called the Spitalwell spring to overflow or flood the field called the Townfield'. Sections of the Broadsike seem to have been straightened in the past to improve the flow of water, and the drainage of the land in large parts of the medieval East Field. Later known as the Canker Dike, the water is now piped underground.

The source of the Broadsike.

The Soils - their qualities and how they are used

The characteristics of a soil come from the underlying parent rock and those of Mirfield vary in quality. This influences how the land where they occur can best be used, whether for growing crops or pasture. The more gritty and well drained soil is found over the sandstone and so provides good land for cereal and other crops. It was on these soil areas that the first large medieval arable fields were situated in Mirfield, the West Field, the original East Field and that probably known as the Overfield. The latter name is uncertain, but it was situated between Crossley Hill and Shillbank. The soils deriving from the underlying clays and shales have finer particles and drain less well and tend to be heavy and sticky and can become waterlogged. These are areas that are more suitable for pasture. The most exposed area with this type of soil was Mirfield Moor. This was the extensive common grazing land for the township in medieval times and until the enclosure of the commons. The soil over the alluvial brickearth is stony and clayey, but fairly well drained. An extensive area of arable field land to the south and east of Northorpe is on this type of soil. On the lowlands the silty and fertile alluvial soils are damp and, as the water table not far below the ground surface, are liable to flooding in wet weather. This land provide lush grass for hay meadows and pasture and in the wettest parts a carr vegetation of alder and willow used for wattle panels and baskets. It was probably by improving the drainage that parts of these soil areas became the fertile arable field land of the Netherholme below Earthorpe and the extended great Eastfield.

This then is the physical environment where people have lived since the last Ice Age. For the last ten thousand years the climate has been moderate, though with long term variations in the degree of warmth and wetness. Here the natural vegetation is woodland, and its clearance has been the result of human activity. The environment and climate have influenced that activity, the choice for places to make settlements, the farms and hamlets, and how to use the land to support themselves. Human activity changes the landscape and that activity is recorded in the places of settlement, the villages, farms, the size and shape of fields, the hedges, banks and ditches and the field paths and roads. People in the past created the pattern of an older landscape in Mirfield, one which still influences the layout of the area today.

CHAPTER TWO

Before History to 1066

Abuot 11,500 years ago, as the last Ice Age finally came to an end, hunters were appearing on this landscape following the herds of reindeer and other deer that moved to summer grazing on the Pennine uplands. From that time onwards 10,000 years of human activity began for which nothing is written to inform us about Mirfield, a name that first emerges in Domesday Book in 1086 AD.

During the coldest phase of the last Ice Age the Calder valley had been on the southern edge of the ice that covered much of northern Britain. It had been a cold and wind swept, sub arctic tundra where the ground thawed at the surface in summer. There was a sparse vegetation of mosses, short, wiry grass and small, hardy shrubs such as bilberry and dwarf willow on thawed ground. There were reindeer, elk (giant deer), wild horse, brown bear, mountain hare and arctic fox. Howver, very few people, if any, had come this far north even thirteen thousand years ago. The present warm climatic period began, about 11,5,00 years ago and gradually meadow grasses, heathers, hazel shrubs and birch and pine trees replaced the more arctic species. There were now auroch (wild cattle), red deer and roe deer and wild pig and in the marshy lowlands near the river the lagoons, fringed with reeds and willows, were a habitat for wildfowl.

As the climate continued to warm, trees such as elm, oak, lime and alder began to spread from warmer regions to the south. It was during this rapidly warming, moist period that thick woodland spread over much of this landscape; trees which had first appeared in the sheltered, lowlands spread onto the higher parts of the Pennines. There was good hunting here, wild boar in the woodland, deer on the woodland fringes, and plenty of wild foods, roots, nuts and berries on the wooded slopes above the river and wild fowl on the marshes and fish in the river.

Hunting, Fishing and Foraging

Since those first hunters appeared people have been present on this landscape, one that changed as the climate warmed and as a result of human intervention. There were people of the Mesolithic or Middle Stone Age who came to hunt and forage

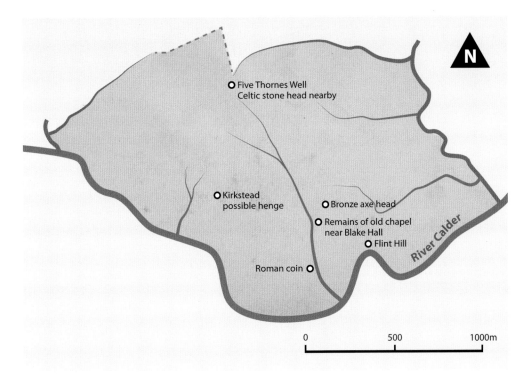

Map showing places where archaeological evidence has been reported.

for wild plant food, making temporary shelters and staying for a short while before moving on as the food supply dwindled, but possibly to return again next year. One of their more permanent camps, was at Star Carr in the Vale of Pickering. This was a large settlement at the edge of a reed fringed lake where the post holes of a circular timber structure, believed to be a house built 10,000 years ago, has been found. Excavation also revealed artefacts made from wood, bone, deer antler and leather and a timber platform which have survived under the peat that now covers the area. Where food could be found for most of the year there were probably other such sites, especially some on the lowlands near rivers, but any such hereabouts would now lie beneath the aluviun that has accumulated due to flooding.

Without any written account, only material remains, the remnants of structures and things that were abandoned, lost, broken and discarded, confirm the presence of people in the remote past. This archaeological evidence is largely missing in Mirfield where few finds have so far been recorded. The map shows where these have been noted or found.

For some four thousand years or more people of the Mesolithic were sometimes here, hunting and foraging food. Their sharp pieces of worked flint, shaped to make axes or tools for cutting and scraping and the tiny flint points or microliths, used as awls or as components of arrow heads, have so far not been reported in Mirfield, but one fragment of a broken, mesolithic flint axe is recorded from Lower Hopton. Such lost or broken and discarded artefacts are often found where soil has been disturbed by ploughing or has been eroded and most can be identified, often by their greyish white colour.

Patches of small chippings of flint, the debris left when striking flakes off a large piece when shaping it into a point or blade, have been interpreted as the sites of Mesolithic camps. Whether such small pieces of worked flint have been found at Flint Hill in Mirfield and so account for the name is not known, but is worth considering. From at least the seventeenth century the name Flint Hill was that of the low ridge of land that ends above the Calder at the southern end of Church Lane. It would have been an ideal site for such a camp. It was well situated for hunting and for foraging for hazel nuts and berries on the wooded slopes above the river, a place where game and wildfowl and fish would be plentiful. Flint is not part of the local geology. Any pieces found in the plough soil would be something to collect, not for its antiquarian interest, but because it was useful. Before safety matches were invented striking pieces of flint together, or on steel, made the sparks to igniting tinder and make fire. In quite recent times it is said of a Pennine shepherd that he claimed to use the flints he found on the moors above Huddersfield, to strike a light for his pipe (Stonehouse, in *Yorkshire Archaeological Journal*, 1994).

Over the thousands of years that the hunter-gathers were occupying the landscape the climate had become warmer than at present and 8,000 thousand years ago average mean temperatures had reached at least 2 degrees centigrade higher than at present.

Small flint blades compared in size to a twenty pence piece.

Sea levels had risen as the ice caps melted and some coastal areas were flooded. The land that is now the southern part of the North Sea was gradually submerged and lost to the hunter gathers who had inhabited it. Britain was finally cut off from the European mainland.

In West Yorkshire people had been making some impact on the landscape. Pollen that has survived in peat from the Pennine moors point to areas where, some six thousand years ago, trees had been replaced by grassy pasture. Clearings with vegetation to attract and then possibly corral wild cattle and deer seem to have been made. People were managing the food supply and perhaps there was some more permanent settlement here.

Evidence from Pollen

In damp conditions peat builds up on ill-drained land such as that on the gritstone of the nearby Pennines. It is from that peat, formed from layers of decayed plant remains, that evidence for the changes in climate and vegetation and also signs of human activity can be traced. Pollen preserved in the peat for many thousands of years is that of the trees and plants that were thriving nearby at the time the layers were forming. Most plants and trees only thrive in certain climatic and environmental conditions and the presence of their pollen in the layers of peat that have built up are indicators of those environmental conditions when the layers were forming. Radiocarbon dating of the successive layers of peat can determine the time they were forming and so when the pollen was deposited there. Pollen studies can also detect signs of human activity by some of the changes in vegetation. A fall in the amount of tree pollen in the peat that coincides with an increase of pollen from the plants which usually grow in pastures or in cultivated ground point to woodland being cleared for agriculture.

A New Stone Age – and the Fairies Ring

Hunting and foraging was gradually replaced by farming in the Neolithic or New Stone Age. A small amount of pollen from cereal plants, found in peat from the lower Calder valley, suggests that some cereal crops were being grown on the fertile lowlands in that part of West Yorkshire about 5,000 years ago. Plots of land were probably being cleared and cultivated for a short time before being abandoned as harvests dwindled when the soil became depleted, and another plot would be cleared. In places where the soils could be easily worked, and where pasture was needed for livestock, domsticated cattle, pigs, sheep and goats, the landscape was becoming more open.

The new types of tools and implements used by these farmer of the Neolithic have not so far been recorded in Mirfield, but that is not proof that there never were any. Two of the most common are the large 'axe' heads (or mattocks) made from polished granite thought to be used for felling trees or possibly breaking up the soil (perhaps both) and leaf shaped, flint arrow heads. The number of finds and the wide distribution of arrow heads suggests that hunting was still important. An axe head made of Lakeland granite found in a ploughed field in Liversedge Park, near the northern boundary of Mirfield is good evidence of Neolithic people in the vicinity about 5,000 years ago, a time when that boundary, a small stream between two townships, was of no significance.

This is a region where much over building, mining, quarrying and intensive cultivation of the land has destroyed much of the archaeology; especially of any of the earthwork monuments characteristic of the Neolithic. The identification on air photographs of the ditches of a large Neolithic henge at Ferrybridge showed that there had been one such monument in this part of West Yorkshire. Excavation revealed that it had been constructed sometime between 5,000 and 4,500 years ago. This was one of several types of 'ritual' earthworks whose function is uncertain. It consisted of a circular ditch with the upcast earth bank on the outside perimeter.

Surprising as it may seem, there is the possibility that there was a Neolithic henge in Mirfield, all trace of which has now gone. The notebooks of the Reverend Joseph Ismay contain two references to a circular earthworks on Knowle Common that was still visible in the mid-eighteenth century when he was vicar of Mirfield. He wrote:

> the vestiges of a Decursorium or Tilt Yard appear between the School and Workhouse. This circus is a large Round Intrenchment with a plain piece of Ground in the middle and a passage into it on either side which the

A leaf shaped arrowhead and disc scraper compared in size to a twenty pence piece.

older people in the parish call 'the Kirkstead' or the 'Fairies Ring'…There is a circular Intrenchment near the free School in Mirfield vulgarly called Kirkstead which very much resembles King Arthur's Round Table but is now almost defaced by ye neighbouring people who have dug about it for stone and entirely spoiled its pristine shape and appearance.

William Turner, writing in the early 19th century, refers to the existence of the Kirkstead, but it is not clear whether he saw it. No subsequent record of it has been found. Ismay's brief description gives no direct information about its size, although his observation that it was possibly a "tilt yard" - an area large enough for medieval knights to exercise on horseback - suggests that the area in the middle of the entrenchment or ditch was quite large. The comparison he makes with the earthwork known as King Arthur's Round Table at Eamont Bridge, near Penrith in Cumbria is of some importance, since he would have seen those earthworks many times when travelling in that area on horseback. That was when he made his annual visits to his family and property at Biglands in Cumbria. King Arthur's Round Table is the fanciful name for the bank, ditch and level area of a late Neolithic henge, which is approximately 300 metres in diameter. It was constructed between 5,000 to 4,500 years ago.

The area between the Knowle and Knowle Lane corresponds to the description 'between the School and the Workhouse', and the term entrenchment would refer to a ditch and an upcast bank. In henges of the type with two entrances into the central area these were usually placed one on the north-west and one opposite on the south east of the circle. An untitled map made prior to the enclosure of the commons in

King Arthur's Round Table at Eamont Bridge, Cumbria, today.

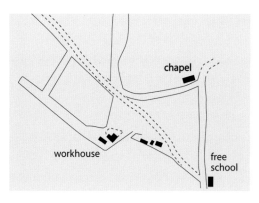 

Left: Knowle Common in 1798. Right: The common as it looks today.

Mirfield, shows the Knowle as an open common with a track across it; possibly through the entrances into the entrenchment and approximately in the directional position commonly found in other henges. Knowle (Old English *cnoll*) was a natural or artificial mound or hill; and a deed dated 1608 refers to an enclosure taken from the common as being 'against the Knowle'. A further shred of evidence is the name Crownest (near to the Knowle). This is a name in use today, but also mentioned in a deed dated 1307 when there was 'half an acre at the Crownest', possibly a name describing the shape of the earthwork seen by Ismay. In the eighteenth century the Kirkstead or Fairies Ring was still an artificial feature on the landscape, whose origin and purpose was unknown but needed an explanation.

As the map shows, the Knowle is now overbuilt and all the evidence for the earthworks that may have been a henge is lost. The possibility of such a site has, however, been included in the Historic Environment Record for West Yorkshire.

The labour of a number of people would have been needed to construct a henge, so it was built by the efforts of a settled community for which we have no other evidence. A few miles down the Calder valley there were people who were using pottery of the Neolithic type and who may have built a rectangular shaped timber house. Excavations in advance of work connected with the water treatment plant at Michael Laithes (near the Dewsbury/Ossett boundary) have recovered grains of spelt and emmer, types of wheat that would be grown by the first farmers (excavation by Northern Archaeological Associates Ltd). That site on the north side of the river is similar in altitude and position to land in Mirfield where, it seems likely, that there were rectangular timber houses, trackways, patches of cultivated land and pasture for animals four and a half thousand years ago.

A Bronze Axe Head – and an unidentified mound

There are no fixed dates for the end of the Neolithic, but the henge builders overlap with the time when the shape of flint and stone impliments changed and metal begins to appear. Flint arrowheads of a different shape, described as barbed and tanged, were now fashioned and their widespread distribution suggests that hunting was still a means of adding to the supply of food. However, it is roughly 3,500 years ago that copper, then the harder copper alloy bronze, began to be used. Bronze daggers, swords and axe heads belong to the Bronze Age when metal began to replace flint and stone.

The only Bronze Age artefact so far recorded in Mirfield is described in the Historic Environment Record for West Yorkshire as 'a haft-flanged bronze axe of Pickering type which might be dated to the middle Bronze Age, about 1400 to 1200 BC'. It was said to have been found in 'made' ground (soil used as infil) between St. Mary's church and Castle Hall Hill. Exactly where it originally came from is not known, but possibly it was nearby. There has been much disturbance of the ground in this area, the site of the medieval castle and, more recently the building of the church in the late nineteenth century. Bronze axe heads are not uncommon finds in and around the Calder valley, some in 'hoards' which it is thought may have belonged to itinerant bronze smiths. The Mirfield axe head is sadly little evidence for the people who were living hereabouts in the Bronze Age, pasturing their animals and cultivating the small plots of land that clustered round the farmsteads.

Between three and four thousand years ago the climate was warm and dry enough for people to live and cultivate land on upland areas that are now often uninhabited. Associated with these Bronze Age people are round burial mounds, barrows, and ring cairns, circular enclosures in which burials or coarse pottery urns with cremated remains are found. These have mostly survived where the land has not been subsequently cultivated. Whether the grass covered cairn or heap of stones on Mirfield Moor, which was seen by Ismay, was of Bronze Age date is doubtful, although it is a possibility. In his notes Ismay says:

0   5 cm

Bronze axe head of Pickering type.

There is a heap of stones upon Mirfield Moor where a person was interred who was denyd Christian burial upon account of his unhappy exit. It is called Tom Fox's Grave.

William Turner refers to this cairn, whilst Pobjoy, who does not give the source of his information, describes the same cairn as a turf-covered mound near Nick House and also says it was called Fox's Grave. There can be several explanations for a mound fitting this description, although the tradition of it being the site of a burial is interesting. Again, a few miles to to the east at Mitchell Laithes, Ossett, an excavation of a round barrow that had been levelled has uncovered pottery urns containing cremated remains. Excavation might have provided the answer to the mound called Fox's Grave but, like the Fairies Ring or Kirkstead, the site has been destroyed by overbuilding.

A Well Populated Landscape

The time when iron appears in the archaeological record, the pre Roman "Iron Age", began about 2,700 years ago (roughly 700BC). The climate had already become cool and wetter and people had abandoned the Pennine uplands. The pollen evidence indicates that there was much less woodland and that more corn was being grown. The archaeology points to a landscape that was more populated with farms and small hamlets of round houses with clay plastered walls and thatched roofs - settlements almost as numerous as villages in more recent historic times. The boundaries of these hamlets and farmsteads and of their rectangular fields and livestock enclosures were all defined by ditches, and inked by lanes with ditches on either side. There were also small drainage gullies under the eaves of the roundhouses. It is these ditches, indicators of the wet climatic conditions, that make it possible to identify many of these sites from the air. In very dry weather ancient ditches, now invisible at ground level, show as patterns of green in yellowing fields of ripening crops. Plants growing on the damper soil over the ditches ripen more slowly and so remain green longer. Over buried walls the reverse process means that crops growing over those are stunted and parched. Only in extremely dry conditions

The upper stone of a 'beehive' shaped hand quern for grinding corn.

when the grass is parched can these patterns be seen in grassland. Air photographs taken over the limited area of open and arable land in Mirfield have not produced any well defined crop marks of this kind, although there are a few, faintly discernable that suggest enclosure in the Crossley area to the west of Primrose Farm.

Excavation of sites identified on air photographs often yields little archaeological material, since most items in everyday use were made from degradable horn, bone, wood and leather. Items made of iron either rusted or were re-melted, much as scrap metal is recycled today. Apart from sherds of handmade pottery, one important item of everyday use found on or near settlement sites are the stones of hand mills (querns) that were used to grind corn to produce flour. The upper, moveable stones of many of these querns were shaped like the old fashioned beehives, round, and tapering towards the top where there was a hole through which grain was fed to be crushed between that stone and the flat, bottom stone. There was also a hole in the side for the wooden handle needed to rotate the upper stone. It is not unusual to find the oddly shaped upper stones used as garden ornaments or in rockeries, put there by the finders and unfortunately removed from there place of origin, presumably a settlement site. Perhaps one or more of these stones will be noted in Mirfield.

A Stone Head – and venerated springs

A sculptured stone head is the one important and unusual item found in Mirfield. It may date from the period of the Roman occupation although it has much to do with the cult of the head favoured by people of the Iron Age. Photographs of it were published in the booklet *Celtic and other Stone Heads* by the late Sidney Jackson of Cartwright Hall Museum, Bradford, but its present whereabouts is unknown. It is one of a number of stone heads found in this part of Yorkshire. The find

Stone head found at Sunnybank.

was said to have been made in a dry stone wall near Sunny Bank Road in 1966. The photographs show a stone head, human on one side and backed by the head of a ram with curled horns, and was described as being ten and a half inches high and made from sandstone. The depictions of a rams head or rams horns together with a human head are thought to represent the warrior god and associated with his attributes of vitality and healing.

The head is a strange object, apparently meant to be free standing and to be seen from all sides. The face has the mustache favoured by 'celtic' Britons, but the dog like rams head might associate it with the Roman god, Mars. Heads (often as skulls) were accorded great significance among the Celts of the Iron Age and were often found associated with springs and other venerated sites. The reputed finding of the head at Sunnybank places it near the now lost spring on Mirfield Moor once known as Five Thorns Well. This was still a public watering place desribed in the Enclosure Award in 1798. The exact site of the spring is now lost but the water may still feed the small pond that formerly provided water for Sunnybank Mill, on the west of Sunnybank Road. Springs have a long history as places associated with healing and many springs became the medieval Holy Wells. Perhaps it is not stretching the evidence too far to suggest that the head may have been associated with the spring, a special place venerated and visited two thousand years ago.

The Roman Occupation – one coin

There is nothing recorded that suggests that there was any significant Roman presence here or major Roman road through the township although there must have been roads and tracks. Other than perhaps the stone head, a coin of the early 4th century AD, the reign of the Emperor Constantine, is all that represents the four hundred years or so of the Roman occupation of Britain. This was reported to be from a garden in Parkfield Way, but as a casual find it may have been lost at any time, even by a most recent owner. There is nothing to show where people were living here during the Roman occupation, of hamlet farms that were still much as they had been in pre Roman times. Timber and wattle round houses inside their wattle fences and farmsteads in ditched enclosures often yield more archaeological evidence for this time, usually

A coin of Constantine compared to a twenty pence piece.

fragments of the mass produced pottery, small bronze coins to use as small change, pins and brooches. This kind of archaeological material is widely distributed in much of south-west Yorkshire and it is hard to belief that some have not been found or remain to be found in Mirfield.

The pollen evidence indicates that more corn was being grown. The population was growing. The Roman military needed corn and requisitioned it from the peasant farmers and a tax was also paid in corn. There were now more regular blocks of rectangular fields identified on air photographs. In some places the fields and roads laid out at this time seem to have survived to influence the layout of the later landscape, although nothing has been noted to suggest that this may have happened here in Mirfield.

The Fifth and Sixth Centuries AD

By the end of the Roman occupation, about 410 AD, there was a change to cooler, more unsettled weather. The demand for corn had lessened as troops were withdrawn from Britain and the pollen evidence seems to confirm that less land was being cultivated. In some pollen samples there is evidence that woodland was now starting to regenerate in some places, and once again the landscape was changing. These were centuries for which there is little evidence; unsettled times when Britain fragmented into small independent kingdoms. One of these was Elmet, a territory approximating to what is now South and West Yorkshire. Along the eastern border of this small kingdom were villages with names like Sherburn in Elmet and Clifford in Elmet. Much of Elmet lay on the coal measures, a geology that naturally supports tracts of woodland, and in the seventh century 'the wood of Elmet' was mentioned by Bede in his History of the *English Church and People*. These were power grabbing times when the British kings, or warlords, vied for power whilst the new Germanic warlords were moving to expand beyond the territories they already controlled. There are also known to have been famines and in the mid-sixth century and an epidemic of bubonic plague, although where and when this struck is not known.

Archaeology has so far provided little evidence for this part of West Yorkshire during the centuries immediately after the Roman occupation. The hamlets where people lived and the sites of any small timber churches and their burial grounds are unidentified; possibly some were on sites that continued to be used in later times. The Romano–British pottery kilns had been abandoned and there seems to have been little hand-made pottery. The coins which had allowed the pottery and other items to be purchased gradually went out of circulation and so much of the evidence for settlement sites is missing. Taxes were paid as food and service to the local overlords. Presumably, the people living here were cultivating the land and rearing the livestock; but were there as many of them as there had once been? Their language was the Old

Welsh, a celtic language that evolved to become modern Welsh. The latin once used for official transactions had mostly gone out of use, except perhaps by those few who were monks or clergy. Christianity had spread in Roman times, and it is fairly certain that the people here were nominally Christian although traditions belonging to pre Christian times had probably not disappeared.

A Change of Language - and the making of a place name

By the beginning of the sixth century the Anglian kings were extending their territories west into the Pennine kingdoms of the Britons. In 627 Elmet was taken, Ceretic the last king, was deposed and Elmet became a region of Anglian Northumbria. The language of the new overlords, an early form of English, would, from that time, begin to influence the language of the Britons here although Anglian people were probably only to be a minority in the population. The old names of places disappeared to be replaced with names of English form. It was probably a long time before the old language of the Britons was lost. Names of natural features on the landscape sometimes survived, some too important to change others of little importance for official purposes. Examples of these are Calder, the 'strong flowing water', and possibly *nant* - meaning 'valley/ stream' - which survived in Nant Ing, a field in the valley to the east of Mirfield church (shown on the plan of the Beaumont estate in 1720). The British name or names for the settlement(s) in what became Mirfield have been lost.

The name Mirfield contains two words that are both probably English. They described this area for those who had to know, no doubt for some official use. The first written form of the name is 'Mirefelt', found in the Domesday Book in 1086. Whether that spelling accurately conveys an earlier pronunciation or spelling is not known. *Feld* was a 'place or open place', unlike modern 'field', which is usually an enclosed area. *Feld* place names are known from the eighth century onwards. It has been suggested that "mir - e' possibly derived from an old english word for 'pleasant or merry' but the description 'the pleasant place' seems a very vague and unhelpful. The best explanation is that it derives from 'mere', that is a marsh or pool. This idea was adopted in the motto on the Mirfield coat of arms ('behold the fruits of the marsh'). Mere, an old english word (-mire being the later Scandinavian) for a pond or pool or wetland seems an apt description of a place where the lowlands in the south and east of it were marshy and prone to flooding before more recent efficient drainage. It is possible that the name Broomer(e) or Browmer(e), a name that was in use from the sixteenth century for land now in Ravensthorpe, may have been a pool or marshy place. Broomer Street marks one side of this area. Possibly then, the name Mirfield described a settlement where there were marshes or pools. There were variations in the spelling of the name throughout medieval times. Mirefelt, Myrefeld and Myrfield, were all ways of spelling the name and there would be differences in pronunciation at different times as dialects changed. However, the area it described had been defined well before the Norman Conquest and has remained the same until recent times.

By the ninth century parts of Yorkshire were seeing new settlers, men of mostly Danish origin and in the areas where they settled there were new place names, probably some places renamed for their new owners. Scandinavian words were added to the vocabulary and many of these words and names are still in use today, including '–thorpes' as in Northorpe, '-ings' (pasture), as Ravens Ing, '-gate' (way or road) as in Towngate and 'syke' - a shallow valley, found in Mirfield in Broadsike, but 'beck' meaning a stream has not been found in Mirfield where the English 'brook' continued to be used. Personal names of Danish type also came into fashion and were still being used locally in Mirfield in the early thirteemth century when Orm and Westmund are recorded. Like the rest of the inhabitants theirs was probably a mixed heritage where ancestors had intermarried with newcomers over millennia. However, it is just possible that there were some whose ancestors had been here when the Fairies Ring was built, if not before. The results of DNA testing have proved that this is true for one person in Cheddar in Somerset today.

Before 1066

Little can be said about the landscape during the six centuries after the Romans abandoned Britain and the Norman Conquest, and pollen studies have nothing to contribute. Mirfield as it then emerged into history in 1086 had been taking on its shape, this defined by the boundaries that it was to have until more recent times. A landscape of wood pasture (open pasture with trees) and marshy lowland. Small farms with patches of cultivation and pasture had somehow and at some time changed to one where there were large arable fields divided into strips cultivated by people who now lived in hamlets. By the eleventh century Mirfield was a township, a unit assessed for its share of the geld, the tax owed to the king. There was a community which cultivated the land according to a shared plan and was responsible for law and order within its boundaries. On the eve of the Norman Conquest that territory was divided between three land lords, each with the land belonging to his manor (house) and there were three small hamlets and probably a church.

CHAPTER THREE

Domesday Book
a snapshot in time

The great survey of England made for the new king, William the Conqueror, had been completed and now it was known who held which lands, their value and so for how much they could be taxed. In the summary made from all the information that had been collected for the Domesday Book, Mirfield emerges into history. One short paragraph provides two snapshots in time, the first of Mirfield before the year 1066, in the days of King Edward the Confessor, and the second at the time of the great survey of 1085/6.

ꝺ **I**n *MIREFELT* . Gerneber . haldene 7 Gamel ħƀr . vɪ . caɼ
træ ad glđ . ubi . ɪɪɪ . caɼ pofſ . cē . Nc̄ hn̄t de Ilƀto . ɪɪɪ . an
glici . Ipſi . ɪɪ . caɼ . 7 vɪ . uilł . 7 ɪɪɪ . borđ cū . ɪɪ . caɼ . Silua
paſt dim̄ leᵛ laɼ . 7 ɪ . leᵛ lḡ . T.R.E . uał . ɪɪɪ . liƀ . m̄ . x . fcł.

The entry translates as follows:

> 3 M.[manors]. In Mirefelt Arnbjorn, Halfdan and Gamal had 6 carucates for tax where three ploughs are possible. Now [1086] three english men have [the manors] from Ilbert. They [have] 2 ploughs, and 6 villagers and 3 smallholders have 2 ploughs. Woodland pasture half league wide and 1 league long. Value in the time of king Edward £3, now 10s.(shillings)'

This was all the official record needed for the vill or township of Mirfield. There were three manors and in the days of King Edward the Confessor, before 1066, these were in the hands of Arnbjorn, Halfdan and Gamal. They were men with Danish names - Halfdan meaning half Dane, Arnbjorn being Arnulf's child and Gamal, meaning 'the elder'. Other entries in the Domesday Book show, all three had other lands and manors in south-west Yorkshire. A manor was a house and all land belonging to it. The three manors might have been of equal size, with land calculated at three ploughs, giving one plough or ploughland each. The ploughland was calculated as being as much land as a plough team (which might be as many as eight oxen) could work in the course of a year, and would vary according to the type of soil. It might be anything between 80 and 100 acres. Possibly there were about 300 acres of ploughed land, only a small proportion of the 2,000 acres of land in the township. The rest was valuable open woodland pasture, possibly about 500 acres and more than 1,000 acres of 'waste' (marsh and scrub moorland). The ploughed land was almost certainly laid out in large areas of township or common fields where land cultivated for the lord's own use, the demesne lands, and the tenants' portions, were intermingled. There is no mention of the number of tenants living on the manors. In 1066 the rents and products of the three manors together had a total value of £3, and the township was assessed for tax at six carucates. A carucate, the latin word for a ploughland, was also used as a unit of taxation.

Twenty years later, following the redistribution of land after the Norman Conquest, Arnbjorn, Halfdan and Gamel had been deprived of their manors in Mirfield. Three unnamed English men were in possession as tenants of Ilbert de Lacy. Perhaps they had previously been under tenants of Arnbjorn, Halfdan and Gamel. Mirfield was now a part of Ilbert's estate known as the Honour of Pontefract. By 1086 there was one more ploughland being cultivated, bringing the total to four (probably 400 acres) half of which was the demesne lands of the manor lords. The other half was apportioned amongst the tenants, six of which were villagers with a good sized holding, probably 30 acres, and three were cottagers with little land. About one fifth of the land was now being used for growing crops, but despite this increase the total value of the manors had fallen to 10 shilling, possibly as the result of reorganization and revaluation after some terrible years.

In 1069 there had been the 'harrying' of the north', a vicious campaign of 'laying waste' to the countryside as reprisals following revolts against the Normans. William had come north and as his army sought out the rebels, villages were burnt and destroyed, people and animals killed. Winter stores were also siezed and famine followed. Just where the worst of these atrocities happened is not certain. Mirfield may have remained relatively unaffected, although for some reason Hopton, like many other places, was said to be 'waste' and of no value.

This was a sparsely populated landscape in 1086, with a very small number of people living within the three square miles of Mirfield township. Domesday Book gives some indication of the population in 1086. There were nine tenant householder , and to these can be added the households living in the three manor halls, perhaps the bailiffs or the tenants. Allowing for four and a half or five persons in every one of these twelve households, or families (as demographers suggest), there would be between fifty to sixty persons. To these might be added another small number - servants or people without land. It seems likely that there were about seventy people, more or less. The manor hamlets were very small each with the manor house and its stables, barns, wash house, kitchen/bakehouse, a yard surrounded by a stockade, and a few tenant tofts (house plots) or cottages. Domesday Book only gives the name of the township, 'Mirefeld', the unit for taxation, and not the names of the hamlets. These were almost certainly those known later as Mirfield (Town or Towngate), Northorpe to the north of it and Ea-thorpe (Earthorpe and now Easthorpe), that by the water or river. Ravensthorpe is a name that first appears in the nineteenth century, a name probably, inspired by the medieval names Ravensbrook (the Spen River), the Ravensbridge and Ravensbridge Lane (now Huddersfield Road).

Of the nine tenant families listed in Domesday Book six had perhaps two bovates or 30 acres, and three would have had only a few acres and worked on the lords demesne lands. They may also have had some trade to follow. All were 'bond' tenants, so not free to leave their land to move elsewhere. They were bound by the customary rules of the manor that were enforced by their lords, the three Englishmen. Two of the manor holders may have been men whose names appear in the early twelfth century. These were Ravenchil and Ketelbern, who were then landholders here. Ravenchil was the ancestor of the de Mirfield family who were major landholders in Mirfield in later medieval times, while Ketelbern was the ancestor of the Fitzwilliam family and his great grandson, William son of (Fitz) William still had Northorpe in the early thirteenth century.

No mention is made in Domesday Book of the number and kinds of livestock kept on the manors, although if the four ploughs did indeed have eight oxen each, then there were possibly 16 oxen belonging to the bond tenants and the same number between the lords of the manors. These are large numbers, but oxen were essential for ploughing and harrowing the soil and were also general purpose animals used for pulling wagons and carts. There were almost certainly sheep, kept for their wool and to provide milk and cheese, a few cattle, goats, pigs and poultry. The only horses would belong to the manor lords,as these were costly animals kept for riding.

Domesday Book provides a picture of life in England in the 11th century, but all that was there in Mirfield in the year of 1066 had been evolving during the previous centuries. During the next four and a half centuries that process continued until Mirfield emerged into the more fully recorded modern period. The basic pattern of the landscape continued to change as need arose, but although the population numbers were to increase they would never exceed a few hundreds.

CHAPTER FOUR

Barons, Knights and Tenants

Being a bond tenant on one of the manors meant you were at the lowest end of the feudal system of landholding. In the pyramid of land holding (tenure) all land belonged to the king, except that belonging to the churches. Barons such as Ilbert de Lacy were the king's chief tenants and, depending on the size of the estates they had been granted, were to maintain a stipulated number of knights for the king's service and give any aid he might need, including money and advice. The barons granted the knights they retained manors and lands in their baronial estates or Honours, one knights fee being land of sufficient value to maintain one knight with his men at arms. Adam son of Swein (Fitzswein), who held Mirfield of the de Lacy Honour of Pontefract in the years between 1130 and 1159, had an estate of lands valued as eight knights. He had to maintain his own men and some, usually the more important tenants in his manors, were his close attendants. Two of these were Ravenchil of Mirfield and Ketilbern who had Northorpe.

Ailric, Swein and Adam son of Swein

Adam was the grandson of Ailric, the thegn who had a manor in Hopton in 1066, but who in 1086 was a tenant holding Hopton from Ilbert de Lacy. Ailric's son Swein was one of the men who prospered under the Normans, and before he died in 1130 he had added more land to that inherited from his father. Some granted to him by King Henry I was in Cumbria, border country sometimes in the hands of the King of Scots. His sons, Adam and Henry, were to hold these lands from the Scot's king, David I. Swein's eldest son, Adam, held Mirfield in the mid-twelfth century. Whether Swein ever had the tenure of Mirfield is not known. Adam also continued to prosper, having landholdings in the Honour of Skipton and others in Lancashire. he also had income from the profits derived the town of Doncaster and the cattle tax of Tynedale, both belonging to the King of Scots. The castle at Mirfield was no doubt important, perhaps a centre from which to oversee all his other lands and manors in south west Yorkshire.

Adam, although of Anglo-Danish family, was most likely Norman in manners, lifestyle and their language, that is Norman French. His daughters, Amabel and Mathilda, were both to marry Normans. Before he died in 1159 Adam had provided for the foundation of the Cluniac Priory at Monk Bretton, so that the monks would pray for the soul of his wife, Maud. He also gave lands and property to the priories at Pontefract, Nostell and to St. Bees and Wetherall in Cumbria. He had also transfered one carucate of his land in Mirfield to Peter de Birkin, his brother in law, and that passed through the marriage of Isabel de Birkin to the Everingham family whose tenants occupied it in medieval times. The land has never been identified, but in 1301 the tenant was Adam de Helay and eventually the tenancy was acquired by the de Mirfields. The heirs of the Everinghams were still returned as holding part of Mirfield of the Honour of Pontefract by knight service in 1509.

Amabel Daughter of Adam - de Crevequer and de Nevile

Adam's heirs were his daughters, Amabel and Mathild, and the former's share included his lands and lordship of Mirfield. Nothing is known of two sons, Alexander and Richard, whose names are found in only one document. it may be that they had died before their father, or were illegitimate. Amabel's first marriage was to Alexander de Crevequer of Redbourne in Lincolnshire. He died in 1164, possibly fighting in Wales where Henry de Lacy was said to have been accompanied by all his knights. Alexander would have to do the military service owed for Amabel's lands. After his death, and with lands held by military service, a marriage would usually have been arranged for Amabel, either by the king or her superior lord at Pontefract. A year later, in 1165, Amabel married William de Nevile. After Amabel's death in 1207 and William de Nevile's in 1211 her estate passed to her eldest daughter, Cecilia de Crevequer, and the younger Sarah, her daughter by William de Nevile. Sarah's share in Mirfield only amounted to 2 bovates (possibly about 30 acres of land) and probably the advowson of the church (see Chapter 7). The fines that were paid to the king for the right to have their inheritance, are recorded in the accounts in the royal exchequer, the Pipe Rolls:

> Sara agreed that she had a reasonable share of her grandfather, Adam's, estate, saving to her half sister, Cecily de Crevequer her right of primogeniture. Cecilia de Crevequer owes £100 and 2 palfreys (riding horses) for having her reasonable part…of all the inheritance of Amabel her mother, wife of William de Nevile, and Simon Fitzwalter (Sarah's husband) and Sarah owe the same for Sara's reasonable part…

Cecilia had married Walter de Nevile, probably of the same family as her stepfarher William de Nevile and Mirfield passed to her son, Alexander de Nevile. There were to be three Alexander de Neviles in Mirfield. Cecilia's son, Alexander, held the lordship until his death before 1227. His son and heir, John, was then still a minor, but nothing more is known of him. He may not have lived until he came of age and must have died before 1230 when Alexander de Nevile II is mentioned. Rather more is known of this Alexander, who died in 1249. In that year an inquisition was held to establish the extent and value of the lands he held by military service and also the name and age of the heir. The inquisition found that:

> for land held by military service of Edmond de Lacy in the vill of Mirfield, 2 carucates in demesne worth 40s. per annum, a mill worth 16 marks per annum, 2 carucates in bondage tenure at 8s. a bovate. £6. 8s. and from free tenants £8 13 9½ Sum £28 18 5½ of which to Edmund de Lacy ½ markper annum and the fees of 2 knights. Remains £28 11 9½ Alexander his heir 12 yrs. and more.

The heir, being under the age of 21 years, was the ward of his overlord, Edmond de Lacy, who would have the 'care and custody' of him and the income from his lands until he came of age. The young Alexander died three years after his father at the age of fifteen. He must have been the only son, as the next heirs were Alexander's five sisters Joan, Ellen, Margery, Julianna and Cecily. Being female heirs and having equal shares each received one fifth less a fifth of the lands and lordship of Mirfield.

Tenants of the Manor

The bond tenants, that is the smallholders and cottagers of Domesday Book, seem to have held their land from the Neviles partly at least for a cash rent. They may also have done labour services for their lord on his demesne, and would also be obliged to attend at the manor court (probably held every three weeks), and to have their corn ground at the lord's mill. Other cash payments would be the 'fine' to 'enter' land as the new tenant, by inheritance or some other way. Fines were also imposed at the manor court for breaking the byelaws and also for permissions for marriages. A 'heriot', usually their best animal, was also paid to the manor lord when they died. The free tenants who are mentioned in the inquisition of 1249 held their land for a cash rent and could convey it to others so long as the transaction was recorded at the manor court. There are very few surviving fragments of manor court records as pieces of parchment stitched together and kept as rolls rarely survive, and all except one are from the fifteenth century. From much fuller rolls of the seventeenth century it would seem that all tenants had certain rights according to the custom of the manor, and these might include the right to pasture animals on the lord's commons (the moor), gather bracken (for bedding or fodder), furze (gorse), and dead wood or turf (all for fires). The valuable timber in the woods belonged to the lord and usually had to be paid for, as were licences to dig for stone or coal. The resources of the manor were valuable and so were carefully protected. A steward often managed the affairs of the manor and presided at the courts. There was also the 'reeve', elected from the tenants, who supervised the day to day work on the land and made sure that tenants conformed to the orders issued by the court. he also reported any wrongdoing to the manor court. Robert the reeve is mentioned in 1219 and Michael before 1304, but after that date no other names have been found.

The de Nevile shield

CHAPTER FIVE

The Castle

Very little is known about Mirfield castle. originally an earthwork and timber structure, this conspicuous feature appeared on the landscape not long after 1066. It was not mentioned in Domesday Book, although few castles were. The site chosen for it was on a low ridge above the River Calder where Mirfield church now stands. This was a commanding position with wide views, especially to the east and overlooked a crossing place on the river. It's most impressive features were the mound known as Castle Hall Hill and the deep surrounding ditch that can be seen on the north side of Mirfield church. These remains are described in the Victoria County History of Yorkshire (volume II) as 'a mound 30 feet high with a platform 60 feet in diameter at the top, the surrounding ditch being 25 feet wide'. The original ditch was also about 15 feet deep.

Mirfield Church and its precinct now occupy what was once the castle bailey or yard. The castle was one of a type built after the Conquest in 1066 (the earliest was that at Hastings). These were fortifications that could be rapidly constructed using readily available materials. A steep sided mound or motte was constructed from the soil, clay and stone excavated from a circular ditch (much as children build sand castles). On the levelled area made at the top of the motte was the keep, the most secure place in the castle, a timber tower like structure for which the only access was by a narrow bridge over the ditch and then up steep wooden steps. Adjoining this look out post and strongpoint was the castle yard or bailey enclosed by a strong timber palisade and with a gatehouse entrance and stout gates. Sometimes there was also an outer ditch. In the bailey were other timber buildings, including a large timber hall and other living accommodation, kitchen, store rooms, stables and a smithy.

The castle built at Mirfield followed this arrangement, with the motte positioned at the wider end of a shield shaped bailey, an area which spanned the narrow ridge of ground that approximates in shape and size to the churchyard of the present church. There is no surviving evidence for a defensive ditch around the bailey and probably there was a stout timber palisade that had a gatehouse at the southern end.

Top: The motte, Castle Hall Hill .
Bottom: The ditch from the north side.
There has been some infilling on the south
side.

The plans over the page show a later alteration to the eastern side of the bailey, probably due to the church being extended westwards (see later). The slight flattening of the wesr side of the ditch round the motte,apparently the result of widening Dunbottle Lane, a seventeenth century road. Recently there a section of the boundary wall collapsed into the ditch at this point.

The position occupied by the castle suggests that it had some strategic importance. Possibly it was built soon after 1070 by Ilbert de Lacy after he had taken possession of his lands in Yorkshire in the grim years that followed the 'harrying' of lands in the north in 1069. Mirfield was at the point where there were lands belonging to the de Lacy Honour of Pontefract on both sides of the River Calder, the first place

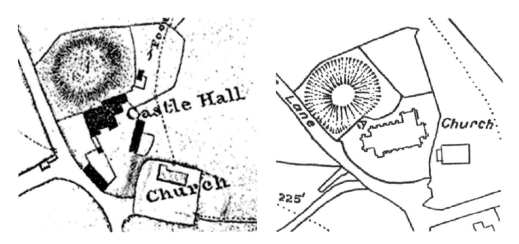

Left: A plan of the site of the castle shown on the Armitage estate plan of 1820.
Right: Plan from the Victoria Country History, the West Riding, volume 2.

west going up the Calder valley where this was so. It was also the place where two corridors of land belonging to the Honour converged, one from the south-west along the Colne valley and one fom the north-west. A castle was also a conspicuous and formidable reminder of the Norman presence. Whether the castle stood on a much earlier defended site is a possibility to which we will never know the answer, since any archaeological evidence must have long since been removed.

Whether the castle was built by Ilbert de Lacy, or later by Adam son of Swein who had the lordship of Mirfield, it was almost certainly there by the middle of the twelfth century. Adam died in 1159, and it is unlikely that it was of a later date. With eight knights fees in the Honour of Pontefract, Adam may have had the keeping of the castle for his de Lacy overlord. Adam's descendants, as holders of the lands and lordship of Mirfield, appear to have lived in the castle, and it presumably functioned as a manor house. However, there is no mention of Alexander de Nevile having a capital messuage (manor house) in the inquisition into the lands he held in Mirfield in 1249, and there is a possibility that it was still considered to be a castle belonging to the Honour of Pontefract. The timber keep and the palisade were never rebuilt with stone. Nevertheless, it was still regarded as a castle in the thirteenth century, the first reference being in 1219 when a document refers to 'a messuage which lies to the north of the castle'. Another mention is in a document signed 'Alexander de Nevile of or from the castle of Mirfield' which can date from no later than 1249.

Mirfield castle was not abandon, as many small castles were, to become an overgrown and lonely feature of the landscape. The hall that had been the centre of activity in the castle, continued in use. With time and many changes the Castle Hall and its outbuildings and gardens was for a time the largest and most high status house in Mirfield.

The Castle Hall

The old house known as Castle Hall stood, until it was demolished, where the hall had always stood in the bailey of the castle. The original hall, was presumably built to the Norman pattern, possibly a part timbered building that may have had lower walls of stone. An outside wooden stair at one end of the building and a stout door at the top was the only access into the large first floor hall that was the centre of daily activity in the castle. Beneath the hall was an undercroft, often without an external door and only slit windows, which served as store rooms and probably was only accessible from the hall above through a trapdoor and ladder. This was the usual style, although no two halls were quite the same, although all had to be made secure. The hall itself was a lofty room open to the rafters with a hearth for the fire in the centre of the floor. Only later would a fireplace be made by a side wall. A raised platform at the far end of the hall, the 'dais', was for the table used by the more important people in the castle and behind this, separated by a wooden partition wall, the solar end of the hall with one or two small rooms or chamber for the use of the custodian's family. Servants and others ate at trestle tables set up in the hall and then cleared to the sides again to make space for the palliases on which to sleep. There were few window openings to light the hall and these were unglazed and closed with wooden shutters, glazed windows coming later. The kitchen and bake ovens would be in separate buildings in the castle yard.

The picture of Castle Hall opposite shows a much larger building than the one described above, but the appearance and proportions of the central part of the frontage suggests the survival of that simple type of hall that was still being built in the thirteenth century. What was probably the medieval first floor hall was much altered by the insertion of the two large windows. Such large windows on the upper floor could only be intended to enhance a big room of some status. Probably a ceiling had been added and two gables seem to have no useful purpose were probably to give a more balanced appearance, matching those of later building phases. The rather small windows and the unimposing doorway on the ground floor suggest the conversion of a large undercroft storage space into small ground floor rooms. The small gabled extension with a side door, shown on the extreme left of this frontage, was possibly built to accommodate a stair that replaced the original outside one. A larger jutting wing on the right, at the solar end of the hall, may be an extension for parlours, or chambers. Many alterations to improve and extend the house had resulted in the

A painting of Castle Hall before it was demolished in the latter part of the nineteenth century, showing it with stone ground floor and timber-framing above.

unusual and much larger building shown in the painting. This was the house described as the 'Capital Messuage of the Manor of Castle', conveyed to John Beaumont in 1519, and an inscription on the woodwork was said to read TB 1522 (probably JB). John Beaumont was probably responsible for some at least of the refurbishing of this largely half-timbered house in the sixteenth century. After a long history as a building of status, Castle Hall was leased as a farmhouse and before demolition was an inn known as the Beaumont Arms.

The Coney Garth

To the north of the castle a field named Coney Garth is shown on the 1720 plan of the Castle Hall estate. This is now part of the burial ground to the north of the church. From Norman times, when coneys (only young coneys were called rabbits), had been introduced into England, coney garths (enclosures or warrens) had been made for these new and exotic animals. A coney garth provided a supply of fresh meat which was highly prized, like venison, and only eaten by the wealthy who lived in the castles or manor houses.

The coney garth belonging to the castle was most likely enclosed by a timber palisade, possibly topping an earth bank. Mounds of loose earth were built inside the enclosure to encouraged these newly imported coneys to make burrows and breed. Usually, a 'warrener' was employed to keep and protect this valuable asset. The coney garth belonging to the castle could have been made at any time after the early twelfth century, but by the seventeenth century it had gone out of use. By that time a 'warren', as it was then called, had been establish on Mirfield Moor. The name Warren House is still used, originally for the home of the warrener. The warren was by then a commercial operation, leased to a tenant by the then lords of the manor. Rabbits had become a profitable business, and among other things there was a demand for their fur by the makers of felt hats.

Was there a Medieval Deer Park?

A park was an important asset for any castle or manor house in medieval times, and there is slight evidence for a small park near the north-east boundary of the township. The enclosing of land within a large ditch and a bank topped by a high wooden fence, the 'pale', kept deer inside a park (mainly roe deer). Parks were of many sizes and were a display of status, but it was also an important source of meat for the household, and besides deer there were also game birds to be had. Sometimes a park was near the castle or manor house, although it might be at the edge of the estate in an area with woodland cover and grazing.

An area that may have been a small park enclosed by a curved boundary is shown on Harling's map to the south of the Finching Dike. Lengths of the boundary are clearly visible from the air and there are still some traces of a slight bank and ditch on the ground, although the eastern section as it appears on Harling's map has been destroyed by a railway cutting. Alongside and above the Finching Dyke, which forms the northern boundary of the area, is a substantial bank marked by a more recently planted double hedge Although no written record of a park has been found Ismay knew the lane leading to this part of the township as Pale Lane (now Primrose Lane), suggesting that this may have been the way leading to the park pale around and by gate into the enclosure. Public footpaths follow what may have been the boundary of what may have been a park. Three field names inside the boundary are named Park Close and Cockshutt, the latter supposed to refer to places where woodcock were driven into nets and caught.

If this land was enclosed for a park it was for a small one, possibly about fifty acres. It may have been in use for only a short time and was probably not maintained after the death of Alexander de Nevile II in 1249, after which the de Nevile holding was fragmented between several landholders. As Harling's map shows, the land was eventually divided into small fields, and melting snow one winter revealed a pattern of rig and furrow that shows the land had been ploughed at some time in the past.

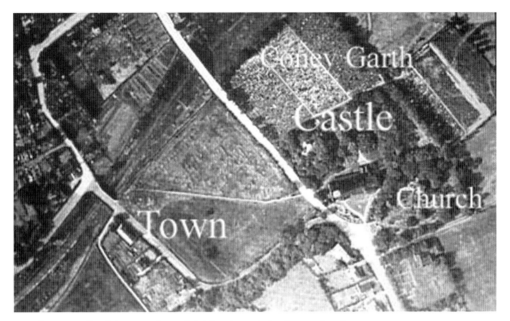

Air photograph of the site of Mirfield Castle and the Coney Garth.

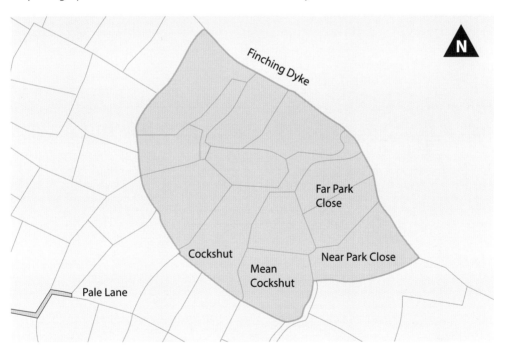

Likely position of the deer park, indicated by Pale Lane and field boundaries.

CHAPTER SIX

The Church and Rectory

The first reference to the church is in 1247 when, in the register of Archbishop Grey of York, it was recorded that 'Richard le Vavasour has the church of Mirfield'. It is likely, however, that there was a church before the Norman Conquest, the evidence being a metre high, sculptured stone that is now displayed in the Lady Chapel in St. Mary's Church. This carved stone with its curious design had been made to mark the grave of a person of some importance, and by the style is thought to belong to the eleventh century. It would have been placed in a consecrated burial ground attached to a church, which may itself have been a dependency of a mother church elsewhere. It would not, however, belong to a private manorial chapel. The drawing

a   *b*   MIRFIELD   *c*   *d*

The drawing taken from the booklet by W.G. Collingwood, 'Angles, Danes and Norse in the Huddersfield district', showing the sculpture on all four sides of this weathered stone.

Left: The headstone. Right: Side view.

of it reproduced here is taken from the booklet by W.G. Collingwood, *Angles, Danes and Norse in the Huddersfield District* clearly shows the sculpture on all four sides of this weathered stone.

There is only a painting to suggest that at the end of the twelfth century, a time when many churches were being built or rebuilt, that Mirfield had a new church. That church was probably built in the lifetime of Amabel, daughter of Adam, and her husband William de Nevile, and would stand to the east of the castle, outside the bailey, until it was demolished in the early nineteenth century.

The painting made of the church before it was rebuilt in 1826 shows an old, steep-roofed building that had undergone centuries of repairs and renovation. The view from the south-east side shows the large, rectangular east window and those of the nave that, without more detail, seem to be of the seventeenth century. Renovations of that date apparently included the building of galleries to provide more seating. The original windows were probably narrow lancets

Mirfield old church.

similar to the two lancet shaped windows shown in the south wall of the chancel; those would be in the late eleventh or early twelfth century style. The small windows high up in the wall of the nave may have been inserted to allow light for a gallery. The south doorway in the chancel appears to be in late Norman style with a series of sculptured orders (arches within arches), possibly with a zigzag pattern in relief, and probably no later in date than the late twelfth century. It is a very ornate doorway for a south doorway into the chancel. Unfortunately, the porch obscures the view of the doorway into the nave.

Confirmation of a building dating from around 1200 is a pillar, now rebuilt against a wall in the vestry of the present church. This probably was one of two or three supporting pillars of an arcade of arches between the nave and a north aisle. Such an aisle is known to have existed (Ismay) and may have been the site for a side chapel, although there is no record of this. The only payment for prayers and masses to be said for the donor, possibly at a separate altar, is that of Sir Robert Nevile of Liversedge who gave '7d. for a priest to say mass' (Chantry Survey).

The tower of the medieval church survives and has been partly rebuilt and consolidated to preserve it. Only the first two stories are of the original tower, which was built with random sandstone blocks and large quoin stones at the corners. Some are very large irregular where they show at present ground level.

Left: The tower of the old church today. The belfry storey was rebuilt and the tower consolidated after the rest of the building was demolished. The roof line of the medieval church can be seen on the east side of the tower. Right: A pillar from the old church.

The window in the south wall of the second storey of the tower also suggest a building of a date similar to that noted for the rest of the church. In what was the inner, east wall of the tower is a low, blocked archway that once gave access into the tower from the nave (see next page). This arch may have been rebuilt and only the top part is visible, since the ground level has been raised in recent times.

The earlier church may have been a small, single room building that became the chancel of a new church. The larger church, built around 1200 to accommodate more people, would have required an extension westwards with a new nave and the tower. This may have involved encroaching into the castle bailey, something that would account for the interruption in the otherwise symmetrical shield-shaped perimeter of the bailey at that point. Like most medieval churches the interior would be as colourful as money allowed. The plastered masonry may have had red and ochre yellow and blue designs on pillars, arches and the walls, paintings of saints and stories from the bible. There may even have been a

The blocked tower arch.

'doom', a painting vividly portraying the torments of hell. There seem to have been some windows with painted glass, some at least with the armorial devices of the local families of importance (Whitaker, in Loidis and Elmet). Almost certainly there would be a figure of St. Mary, and possibly other saints. Much would disappear at the Reformation in the sixteenth century, the paintings possibly under coatings of whitewash and any figures of the saints removed. In the seventeenth century there were galleries made for extra seating, pews now being provided for the congregation that had previously had to stand, and large new windows to let in more light than the older lancets.

The church at Mirfield may have been a dependent church in the ancient and extensive parish of Dewsbury until the end of the twelfth century, the time when the new parish church was built. By then there had been centuries when well trodden footpaths that led to the church skirted the ploughed fields and crossed the moor from all parts of the township. Most of those old, well trodden ways still survive today. They can be followed as both less well used pathways and stretches of modern streets and roads.

The Rectory

Richard le Vavasour had been presented to the church of Mirfield in 1245 'auct Concilii', which meant that the Archbishop himself had presented and instituted Richard le Vavasour into it. This would happen if there had been a vacancy for a year, or more likey because the advowson (the right to present a rector to the church) was in dispute and the matter had not been resolved. Such disputes were not unusual as church livings were valuable and the right to present a rector for institution was treated like any other property and could be given, exchanged or sold. The original owner of the advowson was whoever built and endowed the church and later might be shared like that of Penistone, in which four descendants of Amabel and William de Nevile had a share.

As rector or parson of Mirfield church Richard le Vavasour had the parsonage house, and also any land that belonged to the church, the yearly tithe or tenth of all the produce and livestock to be paid by the parishioners as well as dues such as plough pennies at Easter and altarage (given for services). He was to be the rector for more than thirty years and is mentioned in 1275 when 'Wm de Wetel [bailiff of Morley Wapentake] took from Richard le Vavasour, parson (rector) of Mirfield, 1 mark owed to king Henry (the third) and did not acquit him'.

There was probably at least one more rector before 1297 when John de Heton, an acolyte and not a priest but in minor orders, was presented for 'institution into Mirfield church by Lady Alice de Lacy, custodian of the lands and heir of Thomas de Burgh'. A person who was not a priest could be rector, but a chaplain would then be paid to administer the sacraments. This member of the de Heton family is mentioned as rector of Mirfield in 1301, but died in July 1302. On the 18th of August the following year the Archbishop ordered that 'William de Soothill, priest, be inducted into the church in Mirfield on the presentation of Thomas de Burgh'. An order was issued that 'the servants of ministers of John de Heton, last rector, and the parish to bring in the autumn tithes'. William de Soothill, who had other livings, resigned in 1317 and William de Cressacre, also an acolyte, was presented by Thomas de Burgh. William died in 1346 and was buried in the chancel of the church. It was then that the John de Heton who was lord of the manor of Castle, tried to present the new rector while the de Burgh heir was still a minor in wardship. This appears to have been with the connivance of William de Mirfield, who agreed to go to York to 'support John de Heton in the presentation of his brother, William de Heton, to the church'. He was 'to have expenses of 18d if he could not return the same day'. It was arranged that if the nomination of William de Heton was not accepted, then John de Heton would put forward someone else. If this attempt to seize the advowson was successful then the next presentation would go to William de Mirfield (probably be sold to him). The attempt failed and in October 1347 Queen Philippa, who then held the de Burgh heir in wardship, presented the next rector Ralph de Nottingham. He was followed by John Welgyn.

In 1396 John de Burgh obtained a licence from the crown to give the rectory of Mirfield to the Prioress and Convent of Kirklees and a year later trustees granted them the rectory and 50 acres of land in Mirfield for which a chaplain was to be appointed to pray for the soul of John de Burgh. In 1399 the convent paid £20 to the Royal Hanaper to take possession of the rectory. In the same year Archbishop Scrope's register has this entry dated 23rd August 1399:

> John Welgyn, rector of Mirfeld is stricken with age and debility and John Adewyk, vicar of Ferry Fryston, to act as co-adjutor to make an inventory of his goods and those of the church. Robert. Stokkes, a parishioner, is to assist him in caring for him.

John Wylgyn died in 1400 and the Prioress and Convent of Kirklees then appointed a new rector - William Broughton. He resigned two years later and the income of the rectory was appropriated to the use of the convent. A perpetual vicarage was established at Mirfield and this provided for a vicar with a stipend and some of the dues belonging to the church. He was to serve the church and the parish and have a vicarage house. This seems to have been a small house in Towngate that became the kitchen of the larger house later occupied by the Rev. Joseph Ismay, the house now known as Ivy Lodge.

In November 1539 the Nunnery of Kirklees and its possessions were surrendered into the hands of king Henry VIII's commissioners for the dissolution of the monasteries. The rectory of Mirfield, like all monastic property, was soon leased, and by February 1540 it was in the hands of James Rokeby. Soon afterwards it was sold to Thomas Savile of Clifton for £114. The inquisition made after Thomas Savile's death found that he had 'the Rectory of Mirfield, late of Kirklees Nunnery and a messuage (rectory house) and tithe barn and a close of six acres and tithe of grain and hay and the advowson, held of the king in chief for one tenth of a knights fee, rent 10s 4d value £4 9s

Ivy lodge today.

The Old Rectory (photograph by A.H. Barker).

8d per ann.' He may have renovated the parsonage house where the initials 'T S' are said have been carved on one of the finials of the roof. Thomas Savile died in 1544, found drowned in St. Catherine's dock in London. His son Cuthbert came of age in 1547 and obtained his inheritance. It was recorded:

> For Cuthbert Savile, gent, son and heir of Thomas Savile of Mirfield, gent. who held of Henry VIII, in chief, the Rectory of Mirfield, with lands adjacent, by a twenty fourth part of a knights fee, worth £4 10s. confirmed by Cuthbert aged 21 yrs (Court of Wards,Patent Rolls Edw.VI vol.5).

In 1539 the valuation made of the rectory has a curious reference to the tithe barn in Mirfield: 'In the hands of the prioress, tithe of corn also hay, the tithe barn with close annexed, as it is said, for storing corn or hospitand'. The word *hospitand* means providing hospitality for travellers, something expected of any religious community. After the closure of most of the small religious houses in 1536 the Nunnery at Kirklees had been allowed to continue so that it could provide divine service and hospitality. There was presumably a guest house attached to it, but, as sometimes happened, extra accommodation was needed. How matters were arranged at the tithe barn we will never know, but the nunnery appears to have been recognised as a place providing a service of some importance to travellers.

Traditions – a footnote

Here the evidence for a church at Mirfield since the eleventh century has been set out. The idea that there had been a manorial chapel that once 'stood' at Chappell Well appears in old verse of seventeenth or eighteenth date. Traditions sometimes preserve an element of truth, but there is no supportive archaeological or other evidence that this was so. The spring known as Chappell Well was immediately to the south of Flash Lane where a well (spring) is shown on the first edition (1854) of the 6 inch scale O.S. map. This was in the north-east corner of the most easterly of three closes of land, each named Chapel Well, it was close to the old track leading from the north side of the township to Mirfield church, a footpath that is still a right of way today.

The verse includes a belief that had been passed down for generations that Sir John de Heton had rebuilt the church in 1261. It was claimed that in that year, after a successful appeal to the Pope by Sir John who was in Rome, the manor chapel was granted the status of a parish church for all Mirfield. By implication the chapel was that of his manor, later known as the manor of Castle. However, the church had apparently been rebuilt before that date and had parochial status when Richard le Vavasour became rector. Like many parishes in this part of Yorkshire, Mirfield was probably a dependent church in the ancient and large Dewsbury parish, and was also separated from it at some date that is not recorded. It is possible that the church had been rebuilt when it obtained independent parish status. The events described in the story of the de Heton part in the process of separation tell of a remarkable set of coincidences, and also of the kind of dangers often pleaded when parishioners of a dependent church had to attend a distant parish church. The misfortune said to have happened to Lady de Heton may be the retelling of something that, if it occurred, happened at some earlier time. Whether or not Sir John was in Rome on a pilgrimage is not known, but the appeal to the Pope was unnecessary since the matter of raising the status of any church could be decided by the Archbishop at York.

The first written version of the story is to be found among the manuscripts relating to Kirklees Nunnery in the Armitage of Kirklees Papers where, as a paragraph of latin text it appears to have been inserted amongst other text. There is a footnote in English telling of a confusion in the presentations of rectors between the churches of Mirfield and Kirkheaton which, on the existing evidence, could not have occurred. This footnote seems to have been written sometime in the fifteenth century, and certainly later than 1425, after which the story was entered among the charters relating to the Nunnery.

As a final note, and one that raises questions, is the statement made by Ismay that the remains of a building that may have been a chapel, and coffins and crucifixes had been found in the orchard behind Blake Hall during alterations to the house. This may have been in the eighteenth century, and Ismay does not claim to have seen them.

CHAPTER SEVEN

The Hamlets and Fields

When Henry Harling made the first map of Mirfield township in 1819 more than seven hundred years had elapsd since Mirfield had first been described in Domesday Book. There had been centuries of land clearance and cultivation, of old boundaries removed and new boundaries made when plots of land were combined or divided. The result was a patchwork of fields of all shapes and sizes, small hamlets and scattered farms. It shows a landscape still rural and uncluttered but which, despite the changes, still preserved much of the pattern of the older medieval landscape. That pattern can still be recognized though much less easily after almost two hundred years of change since Harlings map was made.

At the time of the death of Adam Fitzswein, in the mid twelfth century a map of Mirfield, if there had been such a thing, would have looked very different. There would be three hamlets, a castle, a church, large blocks of cultivated field land, meadow, pasture, a large expanse of open moor, all at some time won from the natural woodland.

The settlement that was the centre of the township was the 'ton' or Town of Mirfield situated on rising ground to the west of the Town Brook. To the east, across the brook, was the steep hill at the top of which was the castle. Just how long this small settlement of low, thatched buildings had occupied that site is not known. The position is unusual in this hilly landscape of where the majority of settlements were on the higher ground above the dampness of the wooded valley bottoms. Perhaps a more usual position might have been on the hilltop where the castle had been built. Harling's map shows the hamlet as it as it was in the early nineteenth century, still small and arranged along the west side of the highway known as Towngate and Pinfold Lane. There were few buildings on the east side of the Town Brook where the hillside had probably once been open grazing land until it was enclosed sometime before 1720. A plan of the Castle Hall estate of that date shows that by that time it was the New Closes belonging to Mr. Beaumont. There is no evidence to show that this arrangement of the village had ever been very different even as the village had expanded over the centuries. At the southern end of the village, set alongside the highway (now Pinfold Lane), is shown a

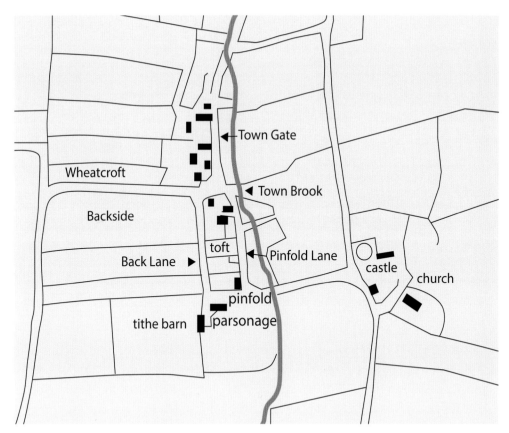

Mirfield Town from from Harling's map of 1819.

row of four, possibly once five, plots of land; probably the medieval tofts or house plots. The surviving boundaries suggest that there may have originally been three plots, all of a similar size, with a further two added later. Each toft would be have sufficient land for a small, probably single roomed house, some small wooden outbuilding and patch to grow vegetables, all inside a boundary ditch and enclosed by a wattle fence. These tofts faced onto the highway and beyond that a strip of open land or 'green' which sloped to the Town Brook. To the rear of the tofts was a lane, shown as Back Lane on the first edition of the 6" to 1 mile Ordnance Survey map of 1854. This separated the house plots from longer strips of land, each approximately one acre, that were probably the crofts belonging each toft. One of these parcels of land is shown as 'Backside' on the 1720 estate plan; 'the backside' was a term used for the croft belonging to a house according to a deed of 1599. To the north of these tofts was the track leading from the western side of the township joining the Towngate, part of the north south highway through the township. Later names for this track were Wheatcroft Lane and then Crowlees Road. This track seems to have crossed the Town Brook and continued up the hill to

51

Towngate before modern developments (photograph by A.H. Barker).

the church and castle and can still be followed in part as a pathway and a road between the Since Harling's map was surveyed much has changed.. The old track to the west side of the township that became Crowlees Road was diverted to its present position as it joins Towngate and Pinfold Lane and two tofts disappeared when the Heaton Lodge – Wortley railway line in was laid in 1901. The line, which ran in a cutting through the village, was crossed by a bridge and cut through the hillside to the east to emerge north of the church. All this construction has gone since the line was abandoned; the cutting has been filled and houses built. Amongst the rearrangements of boundaries, demolition and new building part of the medieval Back Lane still survives and a section of it, now much overgrown, is accessible from the public footpath linking Pinfold Lane to Parker Lane.

Pinfold Lane takes its name from the pinfold that is known to have stood at the southern end near the entrance to the Old Rectory. The pinfold was a strongly fenced or walled enclosure where any farm animals found straying, especially in the corn fields and meadows, were impounded by the pinder. Here they were kept until the owners paid the fines imposed by the manor court. Rounding up the strays was the responsibility of the pinder but nothing is known about how he was appointed or paid. His importance in protecting the growing crops emerges at a much later date in a surviving manor court roll. In 1613 it was ordered that 'all persons with land in the 'fields of Mirfield [were] to pay the pinder 2 pence yearly for each acre, and that the pinder shall be find 5 shillings if he allows any crops to be lost by his carelessness'.

The site of the Domesday 'manor', (manor house), has not been identified. This would be a 'hall' with barns and outbuildings and, perhaps with a small manorial chapel or the church nearby. One possible place might be on or near that later occupied by Blake Hall but there is no firm evidence to support this suggestion. There was almost certainly a house on or near that site before 1326 when, if the identification derived from a sixteenth century rental in the Savile estate archive is correct; that was the messuage then conveyed to Geoffrey the Baker by the lord of the manor of Castle, Thomas de Heton. Ismay's reference to the discovery of 'the remains of a building that may have been a chapel, and also of 'coffins and crucifixes', in the orchard behind Blake Hall, during building work in or about 1747, is vague, but interesting. Whether there really had been a chapel there cannot be proved, but is not impossible. Of the Hopton family who are known to have rebuilt Blake Hall in the sixteenth century some remained Catholic recusants into the early seventeenth century and it is possibly they maintained a small domestic chapel; but what of the coffins and crucifixes?

What does seem clear is that the castle had taken on the function of a manor house in the thirteenth century when it was occupied by the de Nevile lords who held most of the land in Mirfield. Although an Alexander de Nevile described himself as 'of the castle of Mirfield' the inquisition into his lands in 1249 does not include a capital messuage attached to them. The castle still retained that status belonging to the Honour of Pontefract. The Castle Hall did eventually become the capital messuage of a smaller manor of Mirfield or Castle and in 1581 was conveyed as 'the capital messuage called Castle Hall, formerly by the name of the Manor of Mirfield'.

The Northorpe

To the north of the Town and the castle was a small hamlet situated almost at the foot of the sandstone escarpment and overlooking the alluvial lands that lay between the Ravensbrook and the Calder. This was the Northorpe, a 'manor' house and its cottages, one of the manors of 1066. Belonging to it was the one carucate of land, of which according to an agreement reached in 1219 between Alexander de Nevile and William son of William (FitzWilliam), his great grandfather Ketibern had been the tenant in 1135.

Until fairly recent times 'the Northorpe' was the name used at various times for at least three principal houses in Northorpe hamlet, but the messuage mentioned in 1219, the manor house to which the carucate of land belonged was Northorpe Hall. The old Northorpe Hall seems to have been on the site of the house now known as Northorpe Croft, but which Ismay knew as Northorpe Hall. This was to be known as the Old Hall and a date stone over the door of Northorpe Croft is 1701. That is the date that Ismay gives for the rebuilding (refurbishing) of the house by Josia Sheard who

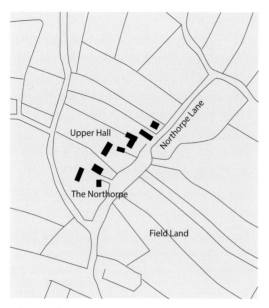

The Northorpe in 1819.

was the tenant at that time. According to Ismay the farmhouse adjoining the old Northorpe Hall was rebuilt in 1704 by Edward Thomas; that is the date on the stone over the kitchen fire place in the present Northorpe Hall: 'ET 1704. This is the house that appears as 'Upper Hall when Edward Thomas paid Land Tax in 1719.

The old Northorpe Hall as shown on Harling's map stood in a triangular shaped piece of land two sides of which are the present Crossley Lane and Northorpe Lane and the third side the common boundary with the present Northorpe Hall. To the north east of the original manor or hall were boundaries which would represent a row of at least four long crofts, each approximately one acre in size, with buildings at or near the end fronting onto Northorpe Lane. Aerial photos suggest that there may have been six of these plots, the toft of the manor. The Upper hall, the present Northorpe Hall, but probably a late medieval house, seems to been built on two of these plots The width of Northorpe Lane, both on Harling's map and today suggests that this was previously the 'green' separating the tofts from the arable field land to

Part of Northorpe Old Hall, showing date stone 1701 over the door .

The present Northorpe Hall (Upper Hall). There is a date stone of 1704 over the fireplace.

Air photo of Northorpe hamlet showing ths site of the Old Hall, Upper Hall and the tofts.
Key: 1 Acre Tofts, 2. Upper Hall, 3. Northorpe Hall, 4. Crossley Lane, 5. Lane to Mirfield Church.

the east. There is no named back lane behind these long plots although Crossley Lane (probably Cross Lane in a sixteenth century document) at the rear of them may have served that purpose. Some parts of Crossley Lane have apparently been altered at a more recent date.

The Ea-thorpe (Earthorpe now Easthorpe)

Near the river but well above the flood plain was the Earthorpe, a hamlet by the water. The later name Earthorpe developed from an Old English word Ea- meaning water. The hamlet was much nearer the water before a change in the course of the river as identified by the field name Dead Eye, an abandoned loop of the river The position occupied by the hamlet best appreciated from the canal towpath to the south of Water Hall.

Earthorpe was probably one of the Domesday manors with the capital messuage. A seventeenth century document refers to the capital messuage of Water Hall 'also called 'the Earthorpe'. Harling's map does not show any boundaries that might be those a row of toft/crofts similar either to those in the Town or Northorpe and possibly the Earthorpe never had that formal arrangement. It was probably a large farm, a hall house with adjacent cottages within its enclosure. To the northwest and west of the hamlet stretched the large area of woodland and moor, some of which remained unenclosed until the end of the eighteenth century. To the south of it were the 'holmes', lowland pasture and field land near the river. It was only in the nineteenth century that the Earthorpe became the thriving centre of the township as a result of its proximity to the turnpike road the canal and then the railway which had attracted industrial and commercial development in the eighteenth and nineteenth centuries.

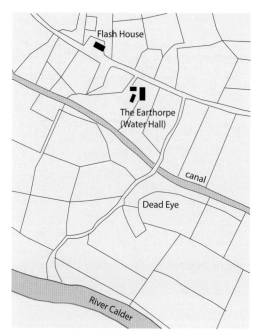

The Earthorpe in 1819.

The Town Fields

For centuries before the Norman Conquest the land in Mirfield was probably cultivated in individual farms with each farmstead surrounded by its own small fields but by the time the records were made for the Domesday Book this had probably changed and a centrally organised system of farming had been established for some time. There are no records for when this reorganisation took place and as no trace of the old farmsteads can be found in the modern landscape; it seems that the new system completely obliterated the old. The medieval system of farming that replaced it has left its mark upon the present landscape and has influenced the way that Mirfield has developed subsequently. The land was now cultivated in large field areas, the town fields, often called the common fields because the land was cultivated in common by all the townspeople, lords and tenants alike. Each of the fields was sub divided into strips, known as selions, that were arranged in groups known as furlongs, in the north sometimes called flatts. The common field selions were allocated to everyone in rotation, possibly, it has been suggested, in the order that the houses stood in the village. if this were the case then it is logical to suppose that the laying out of the settlements and the common fields to a regular pattern was all part of one big organisational change. Sharing the strips of land evenly amongst the community gave everyone a share of the good, poor and indifferent land that was available but each strip within a field, or sometimes within a flatt, was to be sown with the same crop and there was no opportunity for individuality. This was a way of working that needed central organisation and a tenant of the manor was elected each year to hold this position of considerable authority was called the reeve. A document of the year 1218 mentions a tenant known as Robert the reeve who would be responsible for organising the work in the fields at that time.

It is difficult to imagine how the change could be made without loss of production of essential foods as the new fields would have been formed using the best land first, the land most productive land that would be part of the old system. There may originally have been only two fields with a third field added later so that on a three yearly rotation one field could be left fallow to be rested and manured by grazing stock. An agreement made, in 1202, described land as being 'within the fields of Mirfield' and is the earliest surviving record to confirm that the land in Mirfield was divided and worked as town fields. This document also records an exchange of pieces of land, something that was to continue during the following centuries. It also shows that the land was held and worked in acres with each acre being subdivided into two perches and there is rarely mention of within a medieval field system. None of the units of measurement would have been standardised with sizes probably varying according to the quality of the soil.

It is from a court roll of nearly two hundred years later that more information is found about the actual working of the land. In 1485 it was ordered by the manor court that everyone who had not made their dole (boundary) around the sown field before 30th November and around the fallow field before the Annunciation (25 March) was to be fined 4d. Another order in the same year was that everyone was to 'sufficiently repair their defences' of their land and buildings before Martinmas (11 November) or pay 6s 8d. There is, then, surviving documentary for medieval farming in Mirfield but it is also still possible to find evidence of the field land in the present day landscape and to identify three or more of the town's common fields.

Where medieval field land has not been regularly ploughed during the intervening centuries the pattern of the selions is usually still visible on the land surface. A ridged pattern was created because each selion was cultivated by ploughing along its length, turning the soil towards the centre of the strip and so building up a ridge with a furrow on each side. The furrow created a boundary between the selions and assisted drainage. At the end of each furrow the plough team had to swing outwards to achieve the turn and the typical reverse S shape of the selions was created. The resulting distinctive land surface pattern, known as rig and furrow, is one of many features that can be used to identify land that was cultivated in medieval times but other landscape features, field shapes, road patterns, names in use today and those no longer in use but found in old documents must also be considered. Using such various forms of evidence three main areas of medieval arable land have been identified in Mirfield, set around the principal settlement at Town. The three town fields (shown here) formed the basis of a system that had to be continually adapted to meet changing needs and the areas of land shown are the suggested core areas of the original fields before they were extended to meet the need for increased food production. For each of the fields shown on the map a different feature has been predominant in its identification and it is the landscape between Crossley Hill and Flash Lane that is the chief indicator that this was one medieval field land. As there has been little building development there the landscape features are still to be seen and so this area is an important part of the town's landscape archaeology. Hedgerows and boundaries still follow the selion pattern and under certain conditions the selions themselves are visible. On the upper part of the field, at Crossley Hill, slight traces of rig and furrow has been seen in melting snow and during a particularly dry summer and its survival there is good confirmation that other evidence has been correctly interpreted. Each ridge there measures approximately 77 yards (6.5 metres) across, a size that, as medieval measurements were not standardised, is close enough to what was usual in Yorkshire.

The same place in winter when melting snow, lying longest in the furrows, reveals the same pattern. The photographs were taken from the top of Wellhouse Lane just

The Over Field in summer. As the furrows remain wet longer than the ridges so dry weather has revealed a faint trace of the old selions running east west down the slope. Subsequent regular ploughing has gradually flattened the ridged surface and so the pattern is very faint.

The same place in winter when melting snow, lying longest in the furrows, reveals the same pattern. The photographs were taken from the top of Wellhouse Lane just before it becomes a footpath across the fields to join Crossley Lane. That footpath has been known locally as 'the Orgs' or perhaps 'Auks', a name that may possibly be related to the old field system.

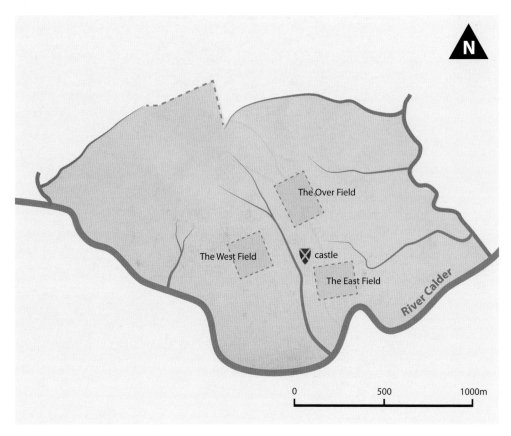

The three core common fields.

before it becomes a footpath across the fields to join Crossley Lane. That footpath has been known locally as 'the Orgs' or perhaps 'Auks', a name that may possibly be related to the old field system.

Near Crossley Farm can be seen some narrow, hedged divisions created when the selions or 'acre' strips of the town fields were consolidated by individual agreement(s) for more efficient and convenient working. These are the visible remnants of some of the piecemeal enclosures that Parson Ismay noted in 1755 when he wrote of agricultural practises in Mirfield 'We have very little common field land. The advantages arising from Inclosures have been long experienced in this Parish'. He enlarges on this with a description of the enclosing hedgerows commenting that 'The Fence is White Thorn and thrives greatly with us, being often cut and kept in repair'. In many parts of Mirfield both Whitethorn (Hawthorn) and Blackthorn hedges still edge the enclosures and are particularly evident at Crossley and eastwards towards Northorpe in the spring and early summer when they are covered with white blossom. The reverse S curve of the selions that has survived enclosure in other areas is not seen here where boundaries seem to have been straightened when land was enclosed.

A photograph taken from the air in the summer of 1997 shows the overall pattern of the medieval field land on Crossley Hill. Of the fields still free from building the central one has been divided by cutting across the long strips but traces of the old boundaries are faintly visible there, continuing those in the field above that are still delineated by hedges and so are clearly visible. Lower down the hill the parallel field boundaries were respected when the roads for Lockwood Avenue, Wellhouse Avenue and Quarry Fields were made.

There is more evidence for the extent of the Over Field at its lower end where, again in melting snow, rig and furrow was revealed in the field to the south of Balderstone Hall. A bank of earth that probably marks the eastern boundary of this lower part of the field can most clearly be seen to the north of Primrose Farm but can be traced southwards where at one point it has been used as the eastern boundary of Balderstone Hall garden, now surmounted by a wall. It seems, therefore, that Balderstone Hall was built on land taken from the core lands of the Over Field. Headlands, the banks of earth created where the oxen turned the plough, can be seen above the houses in Hepworth Drive and behind those on Shilbank Lane where they mark the field's southern boundary.

There is the supporting evidence of later field names that these features seen on the land surface belong in what was once a common field. When parts of the Armitage Estate were sold in 1810 the auction schedule named fields close to Crossley Farm as 'Upper Field Close' and 'Lower Field Close' whilst deeds from about fifteen years later relating to land in the vicinity of Quarry Fields describe it as being part of the Great and Little Field. The use of the words 'field' and 'Close' in these names suggests that they were enclosures created from common field land. Another field in the same area is simply called 'Acre' a name that recalls the size of the medieval land division from which it was formed. For the lower end of the field papers relating to Balderstone Hall give the name 'Long Balks' to the land to the west of the Hall, a name that suggests that lateral boundary banks created by medieval ploughing were visible there.

There is so much landscape evidence for the Over Field that it is disappointing that the name has not been found in medieval documents. The earliest written record of the name does not appear until 1616 when eight selions of land lying in a field called the Over Field were transferred from Thomas Leigh of Stockport and Richard Sonyer of Dewsbury to Thomas Beaumont of Mirfield. Note that the land is being measured in selions although, as there is no evidence to the contrary, it is likely that the eight were, by that date, enclosed into one block. The document did not need to pinpoint the position of the Over Field as this was well known to everyone concerned with the agreement. Four hundred or so years later its location must be deduced since 'Over' means upper, the name is apposite topographically for this field balancing the name Nether (or lower) field, a division of the East Field that lay on the river bank where it is still remembered in a road name. It is, however, impossible to be sure that the correct name has been allocated to this proven town field.

Small sherds of pottery datable to the 14th century have been collected from the part of the Over Field that lies above Quarry Fields, mainly from the area close to the field gate onto Crossley Lane. These tiny fragments may have been delivered onto the field with midden waste taken from the settlements and spread as manure. Whilst of no intrinsic value these tiny fragments that were once part of a medieval household's domestic life have to be proof that the land at Crossley was in use during the fourteenth century. Although other areas of town field land have been searched no medieval finds have been made. In those field areas that are now built over investigation is not usually possible but it may be that such finds could be made in the gardens of houses that have been built on the West Field and on the Kirk Flatts section of the East Field land that is alongside Church Lane.

A photograph taken from the air in the summer of 1997 shows the overall pattern of the medieval field land on Crossley Hill. Of the fields still free from building the central one has been divided by cutting across the long strips (1), but traces of the old boundaries are faintly visible there. They continue ones that are clearly marked by hedges in the field above. Lower down the hill the parallel field boundaries were respected when the roads for Lockwood Avenue, Wellhouse Avenue and Quarry Fields were made.

The West Field

Although the name of the Over Field has been deduced and allocated without documentary proof, for the West Field it is the name that is it's the most significant indication that here was once one of Mirfield's town fields. The name is still in use in the 21st century but is also found in a medieval record. In 1314 William, son of Sabine de Mirfield granted to John son of Roger the Smith of Poterheton: 'an acre of land in Mirfield, that is, one perch of land in Lenethyrholme, between the land of Adam de Deneby on the one side and the land of John son of Richard on the other and a perch of land lying on le Westefeld, between the land of Thomas de Heton on the one side and the land of John de Pontefract on the other'. For this the payment of 'a rose flower' was to be made each year on St John the Baptist's day. The exchange allows another small glimpse into the way the medieval agricultural system worked in Mirfield as it shows that land in different parts of towns field land could be exchanged, in this case the West

Shards of pottery found in the fields.

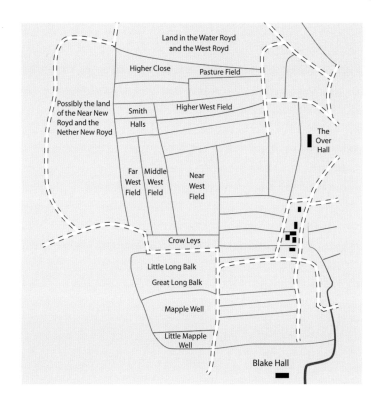

Land in the Water Royd and the West Royd

Higher Close

Pasture Field

Possibly the land of the Near New Royd and the Nether New Royd

Smith Halls

Higher West Field

The Over Hall

Far West Field | Middle West Field

Near West Field

Crow Leys

Little Long Balk

Great Long Balk

Mapple Well

Little Mapple Well

Blake Hall

Names used in the 19th century for enclosures created from the old West Field. The divisions shown are based on those used on Harling's map of 1819 and many of the boundaries then recorded remain in use as roads or as public footpaths.

Field and the Nether, (or Lower) Holme (an area on the river flood plain later simply known as the Holmes), and that the plots were allocated in perches. The fact that the strips of two manorial lords, Thomas de Heton and John de Pontefract, flanked the West Field plot confirms that land allocated to lords and villagers were intermingled.

The land surface of the West Field is covered by the 1960's housing development that has taken its name and so any rig and furrow that may have been visible when the land was being farmed has been destroyed. The roads and public footpaths there do seem to correspond to the tracks that once gave access to its blocks of selions and the names and boundaries taken from 19th century records that are shown on the map of the West Field area (below) indicate that this was once common field land. The Long Balks were well to the south of the area now known as West Fields and the use of that name there in the past shows that the early West Field land probably extended much closer to the river.

Names used in the 19th century for enclosures created from the old West Field. The divisions shown are based on those used on Harling's map of 1819 and many of the boundaries then recorded remain in use as roads or as public footpaths.

The East Field

The strongest evidence for medieval cultivation in the East Field comes from the records of the Parliamentary Enclosure of the Wastes and Commons. In 1798 prominent members of the Mirfield community brought an Act of Parliament that finally erased the medieval field system but, in spite of the early piecemeal enclosure that Parson Ismay noted, the map that was made to illustrate which land was affected shows fields with the names Shillbank Field, Shitternab Field and Netherfield still cultivated and tenanted in strips reminiscent of the old common fields.

It is likely that the name East Field was applied to all the arable land on the eastern side of the township from the church down to the Spen River. The oldest part was probably to the south of the castle and church where aerial photographs, taken before the houses were built on the east side of Church Lane, show slight traces of the stripes of rig and furrow. There, in 1720, a survey made for the Beaumont Estate named the land the Kirk Flatts and so confirms the landscape evidence. As more land was needed the lower lying wetlands to the east were drained to expand the cultivatable area and with this expansion the East Field became so large that individual names seem to have become attached to sections within the whole.

Divisions within the East Field

These fields, or sections of field land, are all situated to the east of the township and so lay within the greater area of the East Field, where such divisions seem to have been necessary because of the huge area it ultimately covered. Shillbank, Shitternab and Netherfield along with North Field, Sonyer Slack and Kirk Flatts are names of subdivisions in use in later centuries when documentary records are more plentiful. Only Sonyer Slack and Shitternab have been found used a document from the medieval period.

The East Field name is first found in a Court Roll from 1594 when the following order was made: 'all persons occupying land adjacent [to] and below the water called the Broade sike in the east field in Mirfield that they scour their ditches in the same before last day of December in pain of 10s'. In the following century the name is found in a deed that described land transferred from Richard Lee to John Nutter as '....one other short butt lyine in the East or nether ffield of Mirfield . . . lying betwixt the Brood Syke and the landes of Gilbert Haldsworth on the [east] and the lands of George Hirst on the west side' was transferred from Richard Lee to John Nutter. (Kirklees).

The most significant evidence for medieval farming on the lower parts of the East Field, and the best evidence for medieval land use in Mirfield as a whole, is found in a document dated 1471 which records that John Northorpe and Thomas Stocks, who were neighbours in Northorpe, agreed to exchange parcels of land in the eastern side of the township and so within the greater East Field area. The document, now in the Calderdale Archives, gives names of many early enclosures and of pre enclosure land but it deals with individual allocations within the larger area and the name Eastfield is never used. The names Sonyer Slack and Shitternab are found in this document and so confirm that names still in use in the 19th century are genuinely medieval in origin and relate to medieval field land rather than being more recent fabrications. As with the Over Field the position of each of these named areas was well known to everyone at the date when the document was created and so there are no indications to enable the precise location of the plots of land named.

Harling's map shows field patterns that may be remnants of strip cultivation in parts of Mirfield other than the main town field areas described. This may be land that was brought into cultivation when climatic conditions made it possible to cultivate land that had formerly been less desirable and when economic conditions made the effort worthwhile. The same indicators that have revealed the main town fields are again used. The document of 1314, mentioned earlier in relation to the name of the Westfield, described '... one perch of land in Lenethyrholme, between the land of Adam de Deneby on the one side and the land of John son of Richard on the other'. The Netherholme lay on the river bank between Ledgard Mill and Shepley Bridge and the description of perches lying between lands of others along with the fact that it was being exchanged for land in the West Field suggests that land there was arable. Land above the Nab could also have been cultivated in the medieval way as field names The Little Long Lands, The Great Long Lands and The Long Close, (Armitage Sale and W R R Deeds) suggest enclosures made from common field land. Their long and narrow appearance supports that possibility and in the Enclosure Award the area is named 'Nab Field'. Below the Nab are the names 'Bankfield' and 'Field Lane' in use today. Peripheral areas of field land such as these would be returned to pasture when the pressure to produce more food had passed and, if they ever were part of the common field system, there is so little surviving evidence that it is likely that the reversion happened at an early date.

These fields, or sections of field land, are all situated to the east of the township and so lay within the greater area of the East Field, where such divisions seem to have been necessary because of the huge area it ultimately covered. Shillbank, Shitternab and Netherfield along with North Field, Sonyer Slack and Kirk Flatts are names of subdivisions in use in later centuries when documentary records are more plentiful. Only Sonyer Slack and Shitternab have been found used a document from the medieval period.

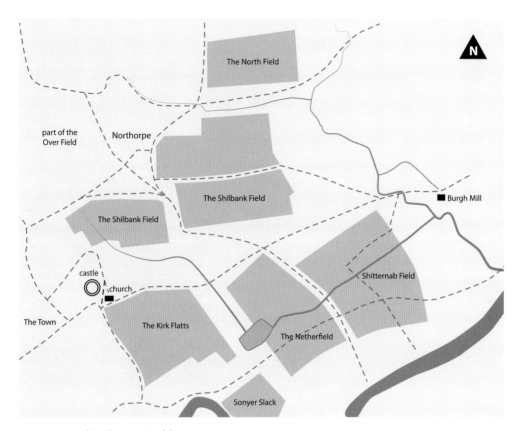

Divisions within the East Field.

The Royd Land

It is clear that Mirfield's Town Fields were extended as and when necessary although it is impossible to say to where their boundaries were at any given date. The oldest core lands of the West Field and the Overfield were certainly extended during the thirteenth century when good weather and so good harvests contributed towards a growth in the population. The process of clearing extra land was known as assarting and evidence available from elsewhere shows that this could be undertaken by the lord or was a matter of individual enterprise by other individuals who could afford the investment of time and money. A payment to the manorial lord was necessary for the licence to take the land and then the process of stubbing out the shrubs, trees and other vegetation and of digging a boundary ditch, around an area that, in Mirfield, could vary in size from one acre up to eighteen, could begin. From the end of the twelfth century to the beginning of the fourteenth and only in this part of West Yorkshire a more specific word, royd, was in use to describe land that had been cleared or rid (ie

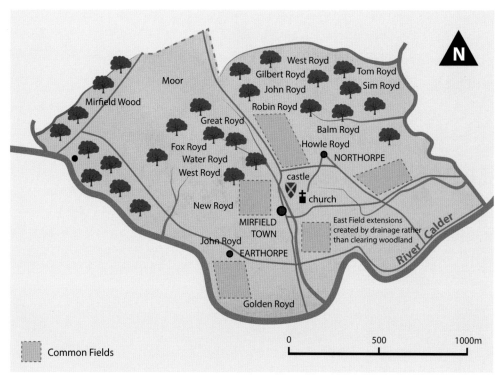

The Royd Land showing areas cleared of woodland.

ridding becomes royding) of woodland or sometimes stones. A record made about the year 1300 shows that this was happening in Mirfield when 'an assart in Mirfield called Benrode' was described as being 'enclosed with certain ditches'. Unfortunately the name Benrode has not survived so, like many other royds whose names have only survived in the written record, its location is unknown. The occurrence of 'royd' in a place name does confirm that here, as in the rest of the country, the population was growing rapidly and where royd land can be identified it does show where clearings were made in what had been woodland. Surviving royd names in Mirfield show that woodland had pressed closely around the margins of the old field land.

Royds often had curved boundaries but royds at the upper end of the West Field, now West Royd and Water Royd, were formed in parallel strips, simply extending the pattern of the West Field acres. Royds of this magnitude that were internally divided into strips for cultivation in the same pattern as the original field land are probably some of those cleared under the instigation of the lord of the manor who would then take a rent from them. A royd named the Great Royd was created on the east side of the West Field and on its western margin may have been the New Royd: These names were in use in the 18th and 19th centuries. No royds have been found to the south of the West Field but Bridge Royd, John Royd and Golden Royd are documented on the river bank. The name of the West Royd was recorded in a contemporary document when that and other royd land would have been a well established part of the Mirfield landscape. In the year 1339 John le Taylour of Mirfield leased to William Fox, also of Mirfield, and Agnes his wife, a plot of land in 'the fields of Mirfield' that was called the 'West riding'. Eighteenth century documents regularly and variously describe the West Royd as being at Crossley and it may be that the West Field 'West ridding' subsequently took the name of a tenant and became the Fox Royd.

Land peripheral to the Overfield was also assarted and it is likely that the Over Field royds covered its entire upper end, from what is now Primrose Farm, on Crossley Lane, to the top of the field at Crossley Common. An earlier name for Primrose Farm was Fieldhead suggesting/implying that this had been the uppermost extent of the core land of the Overfield and that all land beyond was later clearing. A royd adjacent to the Over field was Robin Royd, with John Royd andGilbert Royd. As noted above, the name Westroyd is now associated with the margins of the West Field. Buy the Westroyd also known as Cross Royd lay to the north east of the Overfield ;moving clockwise were Cross Royd, John Royd and Gilbert Royd. There were also to the eastern side of the township were Howleroyds and Balmroyd and Simroyd and Tomroyd on the boundary with Liversedge and Heckmondwike.

The names of some royds names have continued in use; Wateroyd, Foxroyd, Robinroyd and Tomroyd are familiar names in Mirfield today. Names that have fallen out of use are Aldredilrode, Benroyd, Elmitt Royd, Nedsroyd and Pittroid that are found in documents of various dates but cannot be located in the modern landscape. It would seem that Royd names could change over time with a new tenant's name becoming subsequently associated with a clearing and rerplacing its original name. This may be the case with John Royd and Cross Royd; both names that suggest ownership by the Knights of St John. As can be seen from the above map many royd names have been found that apply to land around the Over Field, in Crossley, and it may be that not all of these were in use at the same time. Deceptively there was a fashion in the late nineteenth and early twentieth centuries for using royd in house names resulting in probable red herrings such as Nun Royd, Tan Royd and Oakroyd. Royd names are not found around the low lying East Field land and it is likely that expansion for arable was achieved there by draining wetlands rather than by clearing trees. A 'new dyke' was constructed before 1471 when John Northorpe and Thomas Stocks made the agreement to exchange land there and the 'Newedikehette' (new dike head) was described as part of boundary to the 'Short Weed' (perhaps 'Short Wheat'). 'New' can persist for many centuries as part of a place-name: Newgate, for example, was a newly created highway in the fourteenth century but the name remains in use six hundred years later so it could be that the 'New Dyke' had been dug to drain the low lying land in the south east of the township two hundred or more years earlier, during the same years of expanding population that made royding necessary.

Keeping the low lying lands of the East Field well drained certainly continued to be an issue during the post medieval years when documents are more plentiful. Entries similar to this one that appears in a Savile court roll of 1594 are common throughout the seventeenth and eighteenth centuries: 'persons occupying land adjacent [to] and below the water called the Broade sike in the east field in Mirfield that they scoure their ditches in the same'. The early management of the natural watercourses in this part of Mirfield liberated a large area of land for cultivation by completely reshaping the drainage pattern. Much the man made drainage system is now culverted with the upper Canker Dyke the only visible remnant.

Other Land Use

The particularly rich and fertile soil that is found close to rivers where land is prone to flooding was valuable to the medieval community for the lush grass that it produced. The colourful meadow land was cropped and the mowings stored to feed any animals that were to be kept through the winter, in particular the oxen of the plough team who were hardest worked during the months when there was no fresh growth of grass for them to feed on. In other places, because it was such a valuable part of the economy, meadow land was allocated in 'doles' before the hay was cut but evidence found in three fourteenth century deeds shows that, in Mirfield, at least some of the meadowland belonged to individual holdings rather than being shared in this way. The first, dated 1304, records a grant from Thomas son of Sir John de Heton to Thomas son of Henry de Hopton and his heirs of 'that oxgang of land with messuages buildings and meadows belonging to the same in Mirfield', the second, dated 1326, that John son of Thomas de Heton conveyed 'a toft with a messuage and the buildings seated thereon and in all the land with the meadow and its appurtenances to Geoffrey the baker of Mirfield', and the third, also dated 1326, that 'Joan, daughter of William the smith of Mirfield' made a grant to her father and her mother, Maude, 'for their lives, of a messuage and croft with the buildings thereon, and all the land with the meadow adjoining …'

Obviously not all meadows were by the rivers but not all the land near the river and the Ravensbrook was meadow. The exchange made in 1471 mames lands that were in waterside location There was half a rood of land on the 'Kelderbank' and land in the Colepit flatt was described in the same document as butting upon the Ravensbrook; although the flatt element of the name suggests this should be arable field land. Land on the Holmes, also on the riverbank (described above) would again seem more suitable for pasture but in 1405/6 this too was being measured and exchanged in perches and half acres and was not, apparently, contiguous with any dwelling. The amounts of meadow allocated to any holding in medieval times was small and the Inquisition Post Mortem taken on the death of Thomas de Heton in 1349 does show that, although the demesne of the Manor of Castle had 140 acres of cultivated land, he only had only five acres of meadow.

The Woodland

In the past woodland was a valuable resource farmed and managed, like any other crop, to produce the large timbers needed for building. In medieval times woodland was often protected by a wood bank that has survived in some places to the present day. The wood bank, often surmounted by a thorn hedge, was created in an attempt to prevent grazing animals straying into the woodland where they would feed on fresh young shoots and so prevent regeneration. No trace of any such earthwork has been found in Mirfield but the present day place name 'Stocks Bank' does indicate a place where there may have been managed woodland; in old English the word stocc was used to describe stumps left after the felling of trees. 'The Bank', below where the Community of the Resurrection now stands remains heavily wooded to this day and the steep slope there would preclude that land from other productive uses. As the only written medieval record of a wood in Mirfield comes from the boundary survey made for Kirklees Priory in 1275 (see above) it seems likely that land on the north western boundary of the township was then reserved as an area of managed woodland. The two areas of woodland, that on The Bank and that on the boundary of Kirklees Priory, would have been separated only by a corridor of land cleared to aid safe passage for travellers along the highway towards the crossing of the Nun Brook. Within the managed woodland some trees would be allowed to grow to a large enough size to be used for building. The rest would be felled so that the boles produced the fresh straight growth of spring wood that could be harvested in rotation for use perhaps for light roofing or woven into panels for use as fencing or in wattle and daub walls. No doubt some of the coppiced wood was made into charcoal for use in the iron workings at Cinder Hill.

It is clear from the frequent use of the word 'Royd' in Mirfield place names that shrubs and trees were plentiful but the woodland cleared to enlarge the arable fields was probably not the kind of managed woodland that produced timber for major building work. The moorland landscape encroached by the royds would be one of smaller trees and scrubland but in both cases the taking of timber was under the control of the lord who allowed tenants and freeholders only the right to collect dead wood for fuel. A court roll of 1485 shows the penalties imposed on those who digressed: '. . . for any person cutting [and] carrying away any green trees or any other of the lord's wood, for every offence 4d . . . for any person cutting down thorn trees growing on the moor 12d . . . for any bough 4d'.

Another entry in the same court roll shows that large timbers were being processed in a sawpit. This was a new innovation as no record of the use of a saw pit has been found before the 14th century. The lord kept close control over this new technology and did not intend his use of it to be hindered as he ordered that 'no person obstruct the saw pit before the feast of the Holy Innocents [28 December] on pain of 11d'. No doubt the saw pit was used to cut the timbers that would be used for the building and repair of the West Mills, as was agreed in 1391 when Thomas de Heton leased the mills to Richard Walker, and for other ambitious building projects being undertaken at that time.

The Waste

Any remaining land provided grazing and was a reserve of land which could be brought into cultivation when the need arose. This land was collectively known as 'The Waste' but was far from being that in the modern sense. It covered the largest part of the Township and, as it was a valuable resource, its use was, as always, strictly controlled by the lord. When John Lee occupied 'an encroachment on the wast att Westmyle' in 1389 he was reprimanded at the manor court and fined whilst others illicitly digging pits on the waste to take stone for building and coal for fuel .

Within the waste of Mirfield the medieval documents record pasture and moor land used for feeding livestock In a mid fourteenth century document William de Mirfield claimed against Adam de Heley a fourth part of 200 acres of pasture and 200 acres of moor in Mirfield, making a distinction between pasture and moor but why this distinction was made is not known. It might be expected that pasture was specifically used for grazing. The relative importance of animal husbandry and so the importance of this land probably fluctuated with changing circumstances. Although under the lord's control there was there was the entitlement for ienants to use the Waste, Common Right. Many, if not all, of the inhabitants had customary rights of grazing over what was described as 'the lord's commons or waste'. That grazing rights were attached to specific holdings is show in the Yorkshire Assize Roll for 1219 where it was recorded that Alexander de Nevile had 'unjustly dissiesed [deprived] Adam de Mirfield and Margery his mother of common pasture in Mirfield which pertains to their free tenement'. Grazing for a specific number of animals was allocated to each holding to prevent overgrazing and depasturing' by grazing more than the number designated was, again, a fineable offence for which several court roll entries have survived. Putting diseased animals on the commons was also a finable offence.

Clearings known as greens were made in the waste where a farm was established that probably later developed into a small settlement. Green settlements were probably founded for or by families who followed a trade secondary to their farming commitments. Dewyard Green and Nun Brook Green are names not found until the eighteenth century but Lee Green whose name has remained part of the Mirfield landscape can be traced back to the fourteenth century. The Grengate (Greengate) family held land from the de Mirfield Manor in the 1430's when their relatively newly formed surname had developed as a description of where they lived; by the gate to the green. In 1437 his land and tenement was transfered to Isabel Legh. The Leigh name was alteady known in Mirfield and was recorded in the name Lee Green, theword Leigh, or Lee, meaning the same as "green". A gate to the Green from which the Grengate family took their name, was still in place in 1718 to keep animals from straying into The Town when John Ellis and Samuel Blackburn were paid 1s 0d for setting Lee Green gate post and Joseph Lee was paid 6d for mending Lee Green Gate. Dewyard Green lay to the south of Wellhouse and was surveyed in 1766 as part of the 'Waste Grounds of Mirfield' at 1 acre 3 roods and 28 perches in size by Mr Dyson, a schoolmaster at Clifton, 'by order of Sir George Armitage' but the name may not be medieval in origin. Nun Brook Green at the far west of the township was probably gradually enlarged by clrarances of Mirfield Wood. It is now remembered in the name Green House, first found in 1582 but now more famous for its Bronte connections

The names of some medieval farmers became established in the landscape. In 1719 two closes of land (land enclosed from the town fields) that were part of a transfer to William Turner of Knowle were called Great Jack Bennett and Little Jack Bennett, a name which seems to have survived through 360 years as Johannes (or Jack) Benet and his wife are recorded in the Poll Tax list for Mirfield. The two closes comprised four acres which in medieval Mirfield would have been eight perches of land. Johannes, or Jack, may have exchanged eight of his dispersed perch sized strips from within the town fields with a view to creating the more convenient closes to which his name became affixed. In the same transaction William Turner also received two acres of land in a close called the Great Smith Flatt. This land apparently abutted onto the north west corner of the West Field roydings, close to the Old Grammar School, because in 1608 there was a place there called Smith Flatt Lane. The 'Smith' here recorded may have been William the Smith who was thus described in a document of 1319, or his descendants who, by the time the Poll Tax list was made in 1369 had an established surname: they were Richard Smyth and his wife and Johanna and Thomas who were probably their children. Before the name of William the Smith was associated with land at the Knowle the area was probably called the Crow Nest. This is the name used for the place where, in 1307 Michael de Denby held half an acre of land (ie one perch sized selion) from Cecily de Newmarch at a rent of 12d and so may have been a selion within what, when consolidated and enclosed, became the Smith Flatts.

The Highways

Across the uncultivated land, between the field land, that track ways developed, forming naturally where people passed regularly: to work in the fields, to carry crops to the mill, to go to the church, to visit the castle or manor houses on business, for socialising between the settlements and with neighbouring towns and villages and to linking into the highways used for longer distance travel. Most of these trackways became fixed as the roads in use today whose positions have influenced the modern landscape but then would have been fluid skirting wet areas and puddles and adapting to changes in land boundaries. The basic routes ran north south and east west creating a crossways in the vicinity of the Town and castle. What was known in the 18th century as 'The Great High Road Over the Moor' was part of the way between Barnsley and Bradford and had no doubt been formed in much earlier times The north south route remains today in Pinfold Lane, Towngate and Sunnybank Road although its southernmost part, from Pinfold to the river, was probably rerouted to Church Lane when Blake Hall Park was created The road said to have been used by Lady de Heton on her way to church in Dewsbury was part of a route from there, across what was then the Ravensbrook, passing to the south of the castle and church and then towards the river crossing at Cooper Bridge. This east west route can still be traced as public footpaths but has been superseded by the present Dewsbury to Huddersfield Road which runs much closer to the river and in the past was probably only passable in dry weather. In 1633 it was ordered that the hedges between Ravensbridge and Broomer Gate, and between Ravensbridge and Flint Hill, were to be kept in trim, implying that there were two hedged lanes leading from the Dewsbury boundary to Mirfield Town and church. These two were through routes connecting Mirfield with other places but there were other tracks that connected people within the township. There was a 'way to Mirfield church' from Northorpe that is still a public public footpath, there was a 'a lane from there [Lee Green] to Colepitt at Shillbank' and a trackway at Crossley, skirting the arable land, that lead on to the Moor; this became the northern end of Crossley Lane. The importance of these trackways is emphasised in the orders in the later court that stiles and 'yates', the gates leading from the fields to the waste, are to be maintained and ways left unobstructed.

CHAPTER EIGHT

The de Nevile Manor

For almost a century after the death of Adam FitzSwein, the greater part of Mirfield township was in the hands of the de Neviles. The other separate holdings were the carucate held by Peter de Birkin and inherited by his heirs, the de Everinghams, the two bovates of land inherited by Sarah de Nevile, Amabel's daughter who had married Thomas de Burgh, and the glebe land (that belonging to the church).

By the mid twelfth century the landscape was being opened up. Ploughed land was replacing part of the woodland pasture, the common fields were enlarged and other land cleared for cultivation, some on the edges of the township. The weather favoured this expansion. A warm climatic phase which had begun well before the Norman Conquest continued and at its peak in the 1250s the mean annual temperatures were to be at least 1° centigrade higher than those of the twentieth century. It was important to gain more land from less productive areas, the marginal land. In most places the population was increasing and people needed land to farm to grow their food. There was a growing demand for agricultural produce, and any surplus found a ready market. This was a century of widespread expansion and prosperity.

There were also technical innovations, including the increasing use of the water powered fulling mill that mechanised the laborious finishing process in the making of woollen cloth. Clothmaking was already an important occupation this area, employing a growing number of people. There were also the water-powered bellows and hammers used for the smelting and forging of iron. These increased production and allowed the expansion of iron-making, an industry in which powerful monastic houses such as Fountains Abbey and Byland were creating a monopoly in the south-west of Yorkshire.

Manor lords were profiting from the demand for land and taking advantage of the expanding markets for the surplus that could be produced on the demesne lands. Like other manor lords the Neviles would be increasing their income by granting licences to clear land and the rents then charged for occupying them. There were the profits from their corn mill which was increasingly busy, and probably from the new fulling mill that had been built on the same site. It was during this time that there was also money for building or rebuilding churches.

Mirfield Wood – a settlement on the edge of the township

Mirfield Wood is a name that appears in a boundary survey of 1245, when it was described as being to the south of a piece of land in Hartshead, a position that places it on the north-west side of Mirfield township. It was in this wooded part of the township that two highways converged, one from the valley of the Spen that made its way into the township after crossing the northern boundary on Mirfield Moor, the other was from the east along the Calder valley. These highways were to be increasingly busy. Beyond the Nunbrook in the adjacent township of Clifton, at Kirklees, a priory of Cistercian nuns was established in 1155 and shortly afterwards the Cistercians of Fountains Abbey began their iron production in Bradley on the other side of the Calder. From their grange at Bradley they were to organise the mining of ironstone and smelting iron and then working it a forge built by the river Colne in Kirkheaton. To improve access to these sites they built a bridge across the Calder at the Cowford (Cooper Bridge) not long after 1160, and another across the river Colne (Colne Bridge) before 1185. Well placed where two important highways converged, at the western edge of Mirfield township there was a small hamlet being established with possibly a hostelry and blacksmith as in later times.

It may have been about this time, the late twelfth to the early thirteenth century, that there was some small scale iron-working in or on the edge of Mirfield Wood. Here on the hillside above the confluence of the Calder and the Nun Brook was the one place in the township where the Low Moor Ironstone might be found near the surface, the same band of ironstone that was being mined at Bradley Wood. The evidence comes from the name Cinder Hill, found here as the name of a farm from the seventeenth century until recent times when the name was changed to Mayfield. The name Cinder Hill is often associated with the heaps of ash and slag resulting from smelting ironstone. Wood to make charcoal for smelting iron, ironstone and a good breeze to create a high temperature needed in the small smelting hearths were all to be had at Cinder Hill.

Two local landholders of the period would be aware of the possibility for iron smelting; they were Hugh son of Ravenchil of Mirfield, who granted land in Kirkheaton to the monks of Fountains Abbey on which to build a forge, and his son Adam, who granted them land on which to place a bridgehead for the bridge over the river Colne. We will never know exactly when iron may have been smelted at Cinder Hill, but small scale iron working is known from other places in the thirteenth century. Otherwise it is not until 1319 that a reference to a smith in Mirfield raises another possibility. Whether

William the smith of that date was making iron or was a blacksmith is uncertain since the term smith might be used of either occupation. The document, which refers to William's property, mentions the 'stream which runs by William's forge'. There is the possibility that this was an iron working forge using a water-powered hammer.

The manorial corn mill was almost certainly to be found at this western side of the township by the early thirteenth century. An inquisition made in 1249 after the death of Alexander de Nevile mentions a mill worth 16 marks or £10 13 4d annually (a mark was 13 shillings and 4 pence). This was a considerable asset, being more than a third of the total rental value of the lands and rents and implies that it was a largish mill, probably a corn milll and fulling mill on one site. Fulling mills for thickening loosely woven woollen cloth (see later) were in use by the late twelfth century and as appears later, at the end of the fourteenth century there was both a corn mill and fulling mill belonging to manor of Castle. The materials and labour needed to build the premises, a weir across the river and make the leets to take the water that supplied the power into and out of the mill was an investment that had to be used to best advantage. It was usually the lords of manors who made this investment and took rents paid by the miller and the fuller and a share of the charges made for corn milling and fulling. The site of this mill that came to be known as the Westmills can still be identified by the weir across the river below the John Cotton factory at Nunbrook. The name Mirfield Wood has never been found in any document later than 1245. The land between the northern boundary of the township and the highway was to be cleared to create the common field land known as 'Rattenrawe'. This had probably happened while the demand for land was great and before that demand contracted in the earlier part of the fourteenth century. A document of 1399 refers to the land as a furlong called 'Ratunrawe' (Ratten Row), a name meaning 'the boundary furlong'. West Mills, Nunbrook and Ratten Row, have all been names used for this part of the township.

Crossley – and the Knights Hospitallers

In the north of the township, and forming some of the highest ground, is Crossley Hill. No documentary evidence for the name has been found earlier than the seventeenth century. It seems likely that that the 'ley' part of the name may refer to a 'lee' or 'leigh', open land used for pasture which is found in found in Lee Green; the 'Cross' part most likely identifies it with land and property belonging to the Knights Hospitallers of Saint John of Jerusalem the extent of which is not clear. The land called John Royd, the position of which is indicated in one document, appears to be the same as the Cross Royd that was at the north end of Crossley Lane. Thereabouts was a property said to be at Cross Royd Well or North Bar (Ismay). The well was at the head of Crossley Lane and the bar, was probably the gate onto that part of the moor, the last remnant of it being called Crossley Common. There is no record of how or when the Hospitallers acquired their property in Mirfield, although it could have been early in the thirteenth century. Their Preceptory at Newlands in Normanton had been established in 1189. William de Nevile with the agreement of Alexander, his son, had granted them land in Kirkheaton, presumably after the death of William's wife Amabel in 1207, as she would otherwise have been party to the gift, and before William died in 1211. There there is no record of them making such a grant of land in Mirfield. The Hospitallers, like all religious foundations, were acquiring land from the early thirteenth century and another local benefactor to them was Thomas son of Hugh son of Ughtred (son of Ravenchil of Mirfield) who made them a gift of land in Liversedge.

The only references to their property in Mirfield appear in seventeenth century court rolls of the Knights Hospitallers' manor of Batley, which included property in Mirfield, and was by then in lay hands after the dissolution of the monasteries. Then one of their properties was Nick House and the tenant was Joshua Peel. In his will Joshua mentions 'a common called Crossley', to the north of Nickhouse croft. The court rolls for the manor of Batley also mention other property including an acre of land in Northorpe, which has not been identified. There are also reference from other sources for one enclosure called 'Upper Night (knights?) at Littlemoor and at Fold Head to a house once known as St John's House (Turner). Both of these are at Easthorpe. The original Nick House, like all properties belonging to the Hospitallers was identified as such by the Cross of St John displayed on it. This house was demolished some years ago although the name has also been used of other properties nearby.

Landlords and Tenants

As documents recording land transactions become more common the names of the more important landholders appear at this time. The earliest so far known were those pre Conquest Anglo-Danish names which appeared in Domesday Book. These were replaced by those in Norman style in the twelfth century. The major landholders of part Norman descent were William, Walter, Richard and the fashionable Alexander, and the less well documented, the younger sons Ralph, Henry and Hugh and the women, Amabel, Mathilda and Cicely; all de Neviles. Some of their more important tenants are also recorded, those who later kept the name de Mirfield, descendents of Ravenchil. The changing fashion in names can be followed in this family by the mid twelfth century. Although Ravenchil's eldest son had the older style English name Ughtred the others were of the Norman style, Richard, Roger and Hugh. Their use of the description 'de' or 'of' Mirfield suggests that they were well established here, although they had considerable holdings in other townships. It was Ughtred, Richard and Hugh who granted land in Kirkheaton to the monks of Fountains Abbey. The other known tenant of this period was Ketelbern whose eldest son Godric had an English name; but his grandson was William and his great grandson was William son of William (Fitzwilliam) who released his holding in Mirfield to Alexander de Nevile. Two other men, lesser tenants, mentioned in land transactions around the year 1200 were Wymond who had a son Robert, and a clerk named Peter. and Wulric whose son had the Norman name Robert.

There were as yet no surnames as we know them and all these people had a descriptive name, from which some modern surnames are derived. The more well to do retained the use of 'de' (French for of) attached to their place of origin. For some it established their Norman decent by keeping the Norman - French and. so de Nevile (Nova Ville) translates into the more prosaic English 'of Newtown'. Fitzwilliam instead of 'son of William' was adopted by a landholder of English descent; Norman French was still the language spoken by the aristocracy and knightly families well into the fourteenth century. It would be that spoken at the castle when the de Neviles were in residence there. This was a time when three languages might have been heard in Mirfield, the Middle English of most of the people, almost unintelligible today, Norman French and the latin of the church services and the legal men who wrote the documents.

Very little is known of the lesser tenants the first being William the Tanner whose house is mentioned in a deed of 1202. Most would only appear in records of manor courts (of which there are none for Mirfield in this period) or occasionally in other sources. A few names of Mirfield people have been found in the records of the King's Justices in Eyre (the assize court) at York in 1218-19. Avice, widow of Ranulph of Mirfield, who had the means to attend the court at York, 'accused Henry son of Orm of the death of her husband'. Henry was judged to be guilty, but he had fled and so he was outlawed. This meant that he no longer had any protection under law, could be killed at sight, and his possessions were confiscated. Edusa, widow of Westmund of Mirfield had 'accused Adam son of Durand; of Middleton and also Robert son of Hawise (Avice), his accomplice, for the death of her husband'. The wife of the murdered man had to bring the plea to court, but her plea was abandoned as Edusa had not had enough money to get to the court and anyway Adam had died and so the jurors freed Robert 'since they said he was not suspect'. Adam Kay of Mirfield was also outlawed at the same court for the death of Reginald of Mirfield and it was said 'he has no chattels' (animals and possessions worth confiscating). He too had fled and probably joined with other outlaws to live as best he could. Finally there was William son of Herbert of Thurstonland who accused the reeve of Mirfield, of wounding him. William also did not appear in court to support his plea and so the two who had stood surety for his appearance to make the plea were fined; and the reeve was therefore not arrested. These serious offences had probably been committed over a period of years with the accused, if caught, awaiting in custody at York Castle, for trial in front of the king's justices when eventually they arrived.

The Last of the de Neviles

The Neviles had other lands in Lincolshire and may not always have been in Mirfield. Adam Fitzswein's estates had been divide between two daughters and his daughter Amabel's again between her two daughters. The holding in Mirfield had, however, remained largely intact. After the death of Alexander, the young heir to the Nevile lordship in 1252, his inheritance was divided between his five sisters. The tenants in Mirfield now found themselves to be tenants of one or other of the five landlords. It was a complicated state of affairs about which nothing is clear. It was probably due to the complication of having several landlords that the bond tenancies were converted into freehold rents as appears in later court rolls for the de Heton and de Mirfield manors. Such tenements would now be rent payers, probably no longer owing any work sevices on the demesne and free to convey their holding to others so long as the change was entered in the court rolls. In more recent times freehold rents were represented by the ground rents paid to the Savile lords of the manor.

CHAPTER NINE

A Divided Inheritance
the end to prosperity

In 1253/4 Joan de Nevile and her husband, John de Heton, 'did homage (to the king) for their fifth part of three knight's fees held of the king in chief, as of Pontefract, and took possession in Mirfield.' Joan de Nevile's share in Mirfield was to be known as the Manor of Castle and this stayed in the hands of the de Hetons until the first half of the fifteenth century. Of the other four sisters, Ellen de Nevile, who married William de Pontefract, also settled in Mirfield. Adam de Pontefract, probably their son, enlarged their holding through acquiring some of the other sisters' shares in Mirfield in exchange for land he held in other places. This became another manor in Mirfield and was to become known as the de Mirfield manor.

By the 1250s the landscape would be even more open. Beyond the large areas of the common fields, patterned by the ridges and furrow of the ploughed strips, were the areas of newly cleared land, the assarts enclosed by their ditches and the banks where hedges were beginning to grow. To the south and east of the castle and the church cultivated fields had almost replaced the rank vegetation of the damp and marshy lowlands. Here the new 'fields or 'furlongs' tacked on to the old East Field, were being drained more effectively into the Broadsike. In the north and west of the township was the scrubby moorland hillsides of the common grazing and the remnants of woodland.

At the time of the break-up of the de Nevile estate the population, if it followed the general trend, would still have been growing and so would the demand for food and for more land to plough. The medieval warm spell that made possible the profitable use of less productive areas for cultivation continued, but there were limits to the amount of land that could be cleared if there was to be sufficient common land and pasture left for all the livestock, especially the many sheep whose wool was in demand. At what point, if ever, the limit was reached in Mirfield is not known. The price of food was rising and in 1256 and 1257 there were very wet summers and in 1257/8 a very hard winter when harvests failed and there were reports of famine in some places. The weather pattern had been affected by a massive volcanic eruption thousands of miles away.

The population in the township may have reached around 200 by the early 1300s, although there is no certainty in these numbers. Whatever they were, either slighty more or less, this was a small community with no more than 40 households dispersed among the hamlets and the new, outlying farms.

The Town was the one hamlet that seems to have grown in size as the population increased. On Harling's map the irregular layout of the house plots along the eastern edge of the West Field are probably those of a gradual extension northwards along what is now Towngate. For Northorpe or Earthorpe there is nothing to suggest that these hamlets grew in the same way. However, there is evidence that some tenements had been reduced in size to accommodate another house as was 'that oxang of land with messuages and buildings formerly occupied by Michael the reeve'. In 1304 this oxgang (about 15 acres of land) was granted to Thomas de Hopton 'except for a perch of land with a certain house which Henry de Denton formerly held'. In a deed of 1330 Philip de Brochol granted to Richard de Helay 'a messuage and grange (barn) with half another house thereon'. New holdings were also being established beyond the hamlets, and these were probably new tenements that accounted for the income from free tenants shown in the inquisition of 1249. A few of these new holdings may have been on or near the roydings or on the edges of the common land. One such on the edge of the moor was that of Adam del Leigh mentioned in 1314, probably this holding was on the northern boundary of the West Field (later Lee Green) where Ismay mentions an 'ancient tenement'.

The number of houses on the western side of the township may also have been growing. One would be that occupied by the miller, who usually lived near the mill and possibly one for the fuller. All but the mill were 'free holdings' held for a cash rent to one or other of the lords of the manors. One of these was on the site of the present Yew Tree House, which stands near the A621 road above Nunbrook. During renovations to the house in the 1970s evidence was found for an earlier fourteenth century aisled house on the same site and an archaeological excavation under the floors produced evidence of even earlier occupation with pottery sherds of thirteenth century date (Gilkes). Another may have stood on the site of the old Three Nuns Inn where the remains of a timber-framed building, said to be of fourteenth century date, were found when the old building was demolished in 1939. Unfortunately, there was no detailed account to support this.

One inhabitant in this part of the township in the early fourteenth century was John Fox of Nun Brook who in 1312/4 was to make security for a debt of £20 owing to Sir William Beeston. The certificate merchant guaranteeing the repayment of this large sum of money shows that this was probably a business transaction though what that was is not known.

Life in the Township

This scattered community was bound together by common obligations, being tenants in one or other of the manors. They attended the manor courts and were bound by their decisions. Cultivating their land in the town fields meant adhering to a common plan and cooperation with neighbours. There was also the Christian duty which took them to the parish church on Sundays and holy days. In medieval Mirfield everyone knew everybody.

Most of the people in the township probably never travelled very far, not much further than a weely market or an annual fair in a nearby village or small town. The nearest proper town was Wakefield. Most likely there were a few men who went further, who had been pressed into service with a manor lord or served in the militias when summond for the king's, wars in Wales or Scotland. It was the better off who had need to travel most, men like Adam de Hopton, and, his son, also Adam, and John Fox who all had business with merchants in York. There was also William de Mirfield, probably a lawyer, who went about on official business. There were baronial courts held at Pontefract every three weeks where manor lords or their proxies should attend and with tenancies also in the Manor of Wakefield, Adam de Pontefract and Thomas de Heton were the two. They also attended the Earl of Warenne, lord of the manor of Wakefield, at Conisborough Castle in 1273 where they appear as witnesses to a document.

At a time when most highways were little more than rough tracks, dusty and with hard baked ruts in dry weather or deep in mud with water filled holes in winter, journeys were not something undertaken lightly or for pleasure. Even short journeys were not without their dangers, especially when highways passed through woodland or over stretches of open country. The incident, which was said to have occurred when Lady de Heton was on the short but eventful journey to Dewsbury Church one Christmas day, is one of robbery and a killing at Ravensbridge on the edge of the township. Such events were probably not unusual, even though the full story can be questioned. Outlaws, men outside the protection of the law and often surviving by robbery and using violence were a common danger to travellers.

Most of the things needed by the inhabitants were grown or produced in the township or nearby. Most families, if not all of them, had some land, however little. Some had acres in the common fields as well as a house with a croft and rights to put animals on the common pastures and there were cottagers' smallholdings with a garden and croft where there might be vegetables, poultry and a pig, and possibly they might have a right to put a few animals on the moor. For the people in the hamlets and farms there was a daily round of hard work and, whatever that work was, it would begin at first light in the morning and end when darkness fell. The food supply was dependent on the weather and

The old highway to Dewsbury.

there were seasonal shortages, early spring being the hungry months. Bad weather with too much rain at spring sowing and at harvest time or years of drought could meant poor harvests, shortages of food, of fodder for the livestock and, importantly, for next years seed corn and no surplus to sell. Porridges, of oats or barley, and bread of mixed grains would be the staple food for most and one bad harvest, one year's supply of corn, could mean hunger and malnutrition. Such years of scarcity brought high prices and made life harder and these years were to become more frequent as the climate began to deteriorate.

It has been suggested that about 15 acres of land, and a good harvest could provide enough corn (any type of grain) to support a family for the coming year and there might be a little surplus to sell. There is nothing from which to estimate the acreage of most of the individual holding, in Mirfield in the thirteenth and early fourteenth centuries. One large holding was the 140 acres of demesne belonging to the lord of the Manor of Castle and there were messuages with an oxgang, probably about 15 acres. There were also smallholders who possibly had 4 acres as had a house at Nun Brook at a later time. Cash income, in the form of silver pennies, needed for rents, taxes and any purchases to be made, came from selling produce, or earned by working for one of the more prosperous tenants. Some followed a trade like William the tanner in 1202, Henry the miller, Roger the fuller, the cowherd and the pinder and the baker. One holding apart from the demesne that would need labour was that belonging to Adam de Denby. He had 75 acres of land, 12 acres of. meadow, 2 acres of wood and pasture for 40 oxen, 40 cows, 500 sheep, 80 goats and 80 pig and must have employed a number of people one way or another.

Cottages and Halls

Except for the Castle Hall, all the houses would be of a single storey. Not until the end of medieval period did some of the better houses have a cross wing with upper chambers. Some houses would be larger and more substantially built than others, and many of the cottages of the poorer sort probably only survived two or three generations of use before having to be rebuilt. The houses on the tofts and smallholders cottages having only a single room might have a wattle screen or wooden partition at one end creating another space, sometimes for animals, and a half loft beneath the rafters. Even the best dwellings were damp, draughty, gloomy and chilly. A fire in a hearth at the centre of the beaten earth floor was the place to sit round and be warm and the place where the cooking was done. The smoke curled up to the roof and out through spaces beneath the eves or by a hole in the thatch that might have a suspended hood beneath it. In the majority houses a turf fire smouldered most of the time, except when more heat was needed for the cooking. For most tenants the supply of wood for the fire was often only the dead wood they were allowed to collect, trees or branches could not be cut down and taking the lord's wood without permission was a common offence. A later court roll of 1428 records two tenants selling bundles of wood (brushwood) taken without permission; there was wood to be bought for those who could afford it. Although coal was probably being got from shallow pits there is no mention of it being used as household fuel.

The windows of all houses were unglazed, with only wooden shutters to give protection against the weather. In most cottages a single window and door provided the only light. In these dimly lit rooms the household possessions would be few, a bench, a few stools and a board or trestle table, pallets stuffed with straw or bracken for beds and coarse blankets for bedding. There would be a cooking pot suspended over the fire, in which much of the cooking was done, and a bakestone set by the fire. A shelf or two might hold the storage jars and jugs and mugs of a thick, coarse, brownish glazed pottery. These and a few wooden or pottery bowls and spoons made from horn or wood made up the rest of the household goods. Some cottages offered even less comfort, one such poor flimsy 'hovels' was that of Adam Kay and he had no chattels.

The hall houses of the more prosperous, such as Adam de Hopton, were so called since they had one large room, the hall, and also a smaller room, a chamber/parlour adjoining it and store rooms. Extra space might be provided in some houses by an aisle extension to one long side of the hall. As in the smaller houses, the hearth was in the centre of the beaten earth floor, as at Yew Tree. Stone flagged floors came later and the usual floor covering was a scattering of rushes. The very best house, possibly that of the de Pontefracts, whichever hall that was, might have a kitchen building outside in the yard. The only oven available to most of the inhabitants was probably a stone or clay structure, possibly that belonged to the manor of Castle and used by the baker who would be paid for any baking he did for the tenants. One baker was Geoffrey, who is mentioned in 1326.

In the hall house the usual furnishings were benches and stools, perhaps one or two wooden chairs, a settle with a wooden back. There might be a large table but often trestles or boards could be stacked against the walls when not in use, and any servants often slept in the hall at night. The more private chamber would have stools, a chest, perhaps a small table as well as a bed. The bed could be little more than a wooden frame for a pallet, perhaps filled with feathers, and supported on ropes. The few clothes hung on pegs or were stored in a chest.

The medieval hamlet of Mirfield Town was most unlikely to have the 'black and white' smartness of some villages today. Daub with a surface wash coloured by mixing ochre (dull yellow) or with ox blood (pink) were used in those times and thatches might be sooty and sprouting weeds and grass. The robustness of all these timber framed houses depended on the size and type of the timber and those of the cottages were often flimsy. Walls were thin, only the thickness of wattle panels coated inside and out with a daub made from clay with a binding of chopped straw or sometimes animal dung. Roofs were thatched, mostly with straw, or reeds might be used. Thatched roofs were still common in Mirfield in the eighteenth century (Ismay). Stone for house walls was not used before the later sixteenth century.

By present day standards living conditions for everybody were harsh, unpleasant and insanitary. Fleas, lice and vermin were the common nuisances in all medieval houses, both rich and poor. Cesse pits, dung heaps and middens were the usual means of disposing of sewage and any kind of waste and possibly, as at a later time, the Town Brook was a convenient place for disposal. At a much later manor court in 1584 it was ordered that 'no one throw manure or dead animals or other noxious matter into the torrent called the Town Brook between a place called Dunbottle and the pinfold'. Similarly in 1613 it was ordered that 'no person pollute or throw filth into the Townbrook between Gibhoole and ye pinfold'. From Gib Hole (to the north of Dunbottle) to the pinfold was the stretch apparently polluted by the householders of the Town and may also have been one source of water for their household use. Water came from any nearby useable source, usually springs (wells) and apparently there was a Town Well. The same court roll ordered that 'no person or persons shall corrupt the town well at any time'. Possibly this was a stone lined hollow filling with spring water, but the site is not known. Not all the water was polluted but the thin ale, perhaps milk or buttermilk, were possibly safer than water.

The cold and damp houses, poor sanitation and contaminated water all contributed to ill health and the spread of disease, and the importance of personal hygene seems to have been little understood. Without a plentiful supply of piped water washing of any kind meant fetching it from some source and rarely heating it. The woollen garments that everyone wore were not easily cleaned and any under garments were made of a coarse linen not easily washed. Washable cotton was not known, but there was silk for the wealthy. Infections could easily spread as the cause and the prevention of diseases were not understood and many illnesses could be fatal because of a lack of effective medicines. The inhabitants might suffer from conditions described as contagions, ague or flux. Not infrequently for women might be the fatalities that resulted from complications and infections associated with childbirth, and common childhood diseases were responsible for many premature deaths.

There could also be seasonal malnutrition, common when the food supply dwindled or prices were high after a poor harvest. So how healthy were the people in Mirfield at the end the thirteenth century? Perhaps some or many were and a few survived to a fairly old age. From research done in other places it has been concluded that the lifespan of many people, if they survived childhood and adolescence, might be slightly more than fifty years, at which age people were regarded as 'old'. In Mirfield there is only slight evidence available for life expectancy, and that is from the better off whose access to food and clothing was better than many. Of the de Nevile family, between 1200 and 1250, Alexander I must have died relatively young because his son and heir John was still a minor at the time of his death. John seems never to have inherited, so must have died before his twenty first year. The next heir, Alexander II, died aged about 34 years and his son and heir only survived until his fifteenth year.

Law and Order

Keeping the peace and apprehending wrongdoers was the responsibility of the township. All males over the age of twelve years should be sworn into in a tithing, a group of ten men, each tithing responsible for the good behaviour of its members. An unpaid constable, elected each year, was to arrest any wrongdoers and bring them before the justices for trial at the appropriate courts. Failure to raise the hue and cry and search for or pursue the culprits when a crime had been committed, or to report the offence and bring those responsible before the courts could result in a fine being levied on the township; this is likely to be how it was in Mirfield.

The assault on Roger the fuller of Mirfield at Dewsbury in 1297, mentioned later, and its sequel was of the kind of feuding and violence that was not uncommon. Following an assault on Roger at Dewsbury the story continues when

> Adam de Hopton and Henry, son of John de Heton, Henry le Hunte, Henry the porter and others unknown came with Roger the fuller and broke open the door of William the fuller at Dewsbury and searched his house, they then went to Wodekyrk (Woodkirk) and searched the house of Steven the shepherd where they found William Scot and wounded him. They are to be attached (arrested) and to appear before the tourn.

The tourn was the court dealing with crimes committed in the Manor of Wakefield. Both incidents occurred within the jurisdiction of that manor. Eventually the matter was settled, compromises agreed and compensation paid. It was not unusual for men of some standing such as Adam de Hopton to be involved in menace and violence and breaking the law.

An incident that was sufficiently serious to be the subject of a legal action brought before the king's justices at York. was an act of vandalism, if not one of violence, between the de Hetons and Adam de Pontefract. In 1297 Adam de Pontefract, Sir John's nephew by marriage, entered a plea for damages having

> accused John de Heton and Jordan his brother and Hugh de Heton and Jordan son of William de Thornhill and others for breaking [down] a house at Mirfield. and taking away timber to the value of £10, for which Adam claimed damages to £20.

Although the defendants. claimed that the house was built on their common pasture, a verdict was given in Adam's favour. It is hard to believe that dismantling the timber frame was achieved without some opposition, but violence was commonplace and compensation was seen as a more important outcome as no one was seriously injured or killed.

At that time the cost of building a cottage would probably be less than £4, much less in some cases, and so Adam's house must have been large. Possibly it was to be his new hall or 'manor' house. By now he was increasing his share of the land in Mirfield, and was soon to build a mill for his tenants. His choice of site was, presumably, based on the assumption that as part owner of the lordship of Mirfield he could build on the common land, something only manor lords could do so without permission. Sir John de Heton, also part owner of the lordship, challenged this assumption. How the argument progressed before action was taken we will never know.

William de Mirfield, a lawyer, was also also accused of misconduct. In 1272 it was said that 'William de Mirfield and John de Selby had imprisoned John de Thornhill in the castle [at Pontefract] where he had been sent on the 'king's business'. This was an incident where William took the law into his own hands, perhaps for some personal reason. Unlawful imprisonment was by no means uncommon.

Lawlessness, violence and war were ever present fact of life. When war broke out with the Scots in 1296 more taxes were demanded to raise money for it. Supplies were needed and the sheriff of York was ordered to make requisitions of grain, ale and other commodities, as well as carts and horses and men to transport them to the borderland to the north. Stocks of food that should have been available for the local communities were depleted at a time when prices were already rising. Men were also needed to fight, and by law all able bodied men were required to possess and train to use a weapon, usually a long bow or sword and one man from every family was to come when the militia was mustered for military service. This was a a war that was not far away and its consequences must have been felt.

Sir John de Heton

Sir John de Heton, husband of Joan de Nevile, was one man who survived to a good age for those days; he was more than sixty years old when he died. His modest inheritance had included a tenancy of a manor in Kirkheaton, from which the family took its name, and with his marriage to Joan de Nevile, came control of her lands. There were to be more John de Hetons in Mirfield, but none of the others were apparently knights; Sir John is identified by the use of his title in documents. Whether his knighthood was granted by reason of some military service is not known, but more likely that it was a requirement if he had an income of at least £20 a year. As a knight he would be obliged to serve on juries and perform any official duties assigned to him in the county and possibly do, or pay in lieu of, military service.

In 1265 he came close to losing his lands, if not his life, when he had become involved in the revolt of the northern barons. Whatever part he had played, John and his near neighbour, Sir John de Soothill were listed as 'king's enemies' in 1266, and their lands were assessed before being confiscated. He may have been in the fighting at Northampton where his brother in law by marriage, Adam de Newmarche had been captured, or possibly he was among that part of the rebel force besieged in Kenilworth Castle in 1264 and taken prisoner. His manor at Kirkheaton was assessed before confiscation but, fortunately, the Manor of Castle in Mirfield was not his but held in right of his wife Joan de Nevile. Like many of the rebels, he was eventually pardoned and having been fined retained his lands. In 1275 it was said that 'Ralph de Milford took from the vill of Mirfield 5 shillings owing to king Henry and did not acquit the debtors', but there is nothing to say whether the fine was connected with the rebel activities.

In 1293 another John de Heton became rector of Mirfield. Just what his relationship was to Sir John is not known, despite the claims that this was Sir John's brother. In 1297 both Sir John de Heton and Sir John the Rector were named as landholders in Mirfield, and in 1300 the latter witnessed the deed of exchange between Adam de Pontefract and Sir John de Heton, lord of the manor. It should be pointed out that 'Sir' was a curtesy title also given to priests. Sir John the Rector, died in July1302. Sir John de Heton had been a king's coroner in Yorkshire for a number of years, but in 1300 it was recommended that he be replaced because of his incapacity and infirmity. He must have died before June 1303, because at that date it was his son John who made further agreement with Adam de Pontefract concerning a mill. By this time John, son and heir of Sir John de Heton, was probably well into middle age. So much for a confusion of names!

CHAPTER TEN

The Early 14th Century

By the early fourteenth century most of the land that could be used to grow crops was now being ploughed, and there was a need to have sufficient land left for grazing livestock. The East Field had probably been then extended almost to the boundary of the Ravensbrook, and the Netherfield part to the banks of the Calder, most of which area is now Ravensthorpe. The weather was also becoming cooler and more unsettled, and this meant that harvests were becoming less reliable and food prices rising. In 1305 a hot dry summer in England resulted in a poor harvests and shortages of food, even almost famine in some places. Winters were now colder especially 1309/10 when rivers froze and fires were lit on the frozen river Thames. What had probably been times of prosperity were slowly coming to an end, but not quite yet.

The River

The river should be mentioned, although there are few references to it in any documents. However, by the early fourteenth century it was providing the power not only for corn mills but the new fulling mills, the first industrial development along its banks and the only such until the late eighteenth century. In the mid-eighteenth century, according to Ismay, it was 'a river in which, there are many species of fish, salmon, trout, perch, greyling, gudgeon, daice and eels'. Industrial development and the pollution it caused eventually put an end to this plentiful supply of fish. Whether fish from the river was eaten by all the inhabitants in the township in medieval times is not known. It certainly was in manor houses, some of which had their own fish ponds. Fish could be eaten on Wednesdays and Fridays and other days of fasting in the church calendar when meat was forbidden. The fishing on a river usually belonged to the landholders along its banks, lords of manors who might grant a licence for a tenant to fish. As might be expected there were fines for fishing without licence and fish traps were not uncommon. The river was taken for granted no doubt, it was where boys swam in the summer and sheep were driven from the moor to be washed in summer. On it were slow moving heavy loads, easier and cheaper when cartage along the highways even slower and less easy. There is mention in the Wakefield court rolls to timber having been brought from Raistrick to Wakefield down the river.

There was always the flooding and the damage it caused. As it takes its course through the alluvial levels the Calder at Mirfield has always been prone to flooding and to erosion of its banks. The mills that depended on the water might be stopped for a while in time of drought, but flooding could stop them and cause damage. Tenants of the mills had to be skilled in controlling the flow of water. Even with the risk of flooding the fertile soils of the lowlands was worth cultivating and while the climate was still that of the medieval warm spell and the land was needed that risk had been taken. As the climate deteriorated in the early fourteenth century field land adjacent to the river, such as the Netherholme, must have been even more prone to flooding. Flood prevention in medieval times was probably as it was later, earth banks, or butts, probably made and maintained by occupiers of the land, as they were in the sixteenth century. At a court for the Manor of Castle it was ordered that ' John Hutchinson to make the bank for water at the Sands'.

Mirfield Bridge

By the late twelfth century, if not before, there is likely to have been a bridge across the river at Mirfield. The first reference to one is in 1219, when a piece of land in Hopton was described as extending 'as far as the site of the old bridge'. If this really is a reference to Mirfield Bridge then it implies that by that time the bridge site had been moved and a new structure built. This was not unusual in Mirfield where, on later evidence, flood damage and erosion of the river banks are the reasons given by Ismay for relocating the bridge in the eighteenth century. The next indirect reference to a bridge occurs in 1399, when, on the Mirfield side of the river, half an acre of land in the Netherholme was described as lying between certain lands and ' the banks of the water of the Keldyr and abutting on the east end on Brygloyne' (Bridge Lane). That would place the bridge further up the river than in later times

The bridge at Mirfield was one of the five medieval bridges across the Calder between Wakefield and Brighouse, one at each of those places, and at Horbury, Mirfield and Cowford or Cooper Bridge, otherwise the river was crossed by fords. At Mirfield it was the crossing point for the highway which ran from north to south passing through the then centre of the township, the hamlet, now Towngate. It then followed Blake Hall Lane (later enclosed in Blake Hall Park), and south to cross the river and so to Hopton New Hall eventually to join the old highway from Huddersfield to Barnsley at Liley.

The River Calder. In the foreground on the left of the picture is the probable site of the old bridge.

The medieval bridge was almost certainly a wooden structure needing regular repairs and occasionally being rebuilt. In 1484 Henry Savile, Esq, of Thornhill left five pounds in his will 'for the new bridge at Mirfield'.

The heavy dashed line on the map on the next page shows the old highway through Mirfield and Hopton and the site of the original bridge. This became the highway from Bradford to Barnsley. The line of the road varied as it approached the river from the north when the bridge had to be relocated.

The subsequent history of Mirfield Bridge takes us beyond medieval, times but some mention of it is useful in identifying which of the later bridges was the successor of the medieval crossing. A century and a half after Henry Savile had contributed to the building of the new bridge', in 1640 Mirfield Bridge was in 'great ruyne', and because it was said to be 'very useful to the severall inhabitants of the W[est] R[iding]', the wapentake [of Agbrigg and Morley] raised a hundred pounds (roughly equivalent to eight thousand pounds now) for the repairs By that time the obligation to maintain bridges, other than private bridges, was a public responsibility charged on the division of a county known as a wapentake and repairs were by the orders of local justices of the peace. Seventy seven years later, in 1717 a further eighty pounds (about six thousand pounds now) was needed for repairs and only five years later Mirfield Bridge was said

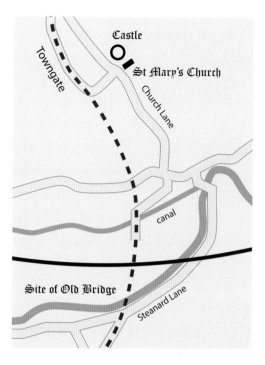

Line of the old highway through Mirfield and across the River Calder.

to be broken down by floods.

A record of the disputes with the West Riding justices of the peace that began in the seventeenth century regarding the responsibility for maintaining a bridge that had been built at Ledgard Mill, was entered in the Mirfield parish registers. It was said that the bridge was built by the Ledgards who were owners of the mill and they who built the bridge and should maintain the bridge. The bridge that was maintained by the wapentake, the authority responsible among other matters for the upkeep of highways and bridges, was the public bridge, and was the bridge refered to in 1713 as 'Mirfield Bridge alias Shepley Bridge' (the Shepleys having occupied the nearby Low Mills). Ledgard's Bridge was first built by the Ledgards in the late sixteenth century, within living memory of local men in 1627. It was eventually recognised as a pubic bridge in 1798, prior to which the responsibility for repairs lay with the owners of Ledgard Mill.

Adam de Pontefract's Mill

Increased demand was no doubt behind Adam de Pontefract investing in a mill. So far the only mills on the river were the manorial ones belonging to Sir John de Heton, eventually known as the West Mills. About the year 1300 in an exchange of land Sir John de Heton released to Adam de Pontefract 'the site of a mill and of a mill pond in le Holme, on the water of Keldir'. The population had been growing and presumably there was enough demand to make the investment in a mill for both fulling cloth and grinding corn worthwhile, and Adam de Pontefract was intent on building a mill to be used by his own tenants. Sir John's manorial mill had enjoyed a monopoly in the township for corn milling and fulling and he apparently secured some rights to the payments charged at the new mill. These rights ended in 1303, shortly after Sir John's death, when Adam de Pontefract made a further agreement with John the son of Sir John, now lord of the Manor of Castle. In return for gaining access to a wood that

Site of the West Mill marked with an arrow.

John had bought in Hopton, he relinquished his agreed payments from the new mill in return for which 'Adam granted to John 'a road 40 feet wide from the wood John had bought in Hopton … to the highroad leading to Mirfield Bridge [which lay] beyond Adam's land, where it [the road] could be fitly made for the water of Calder, for driving all kinds of beasts except goats'. As well as relinquishing his rights in the mill, John de Heton also gave Adam 'leave for a dam for the mill … and leave to repair it and extend it, out of Adam's land so that the road should always be 40 feet wide.

Sheep and Woollen Cloth

There is no mention of the making of woollen cloth in Mirfield in medieval times, although it was certainly a well established industry. The appearance of Roger the fuller of Mirfield at the Manor Court at Wakefield in 1297 is the first direct evidence. By 1331 there were two fullers in Mirfield, Nicholas and John, presumably working the two mills mentioned above. The end product was almost certainly a coarse woollen cloth used for clothing and blankets; the finer woollen cloths were made elsewhere in towns such as York and Lincoln.

The process began with the rearing and shearing sheep. Sheep were mainly kept for their wool, although the ewes milk that was made into cheese and the meat from older animals were also important. There would be many sheep grazing on Mirfield Moor, and other pastures, some belonging to fairly large flocks. In the winter of 1346 Adam de Hopton acquired a large holding that had previously belonged to Adam de Denby, and that included pasture for 500 sheep, the number allowed for that holding on the common grazing or other pasture, and he may also have had more. The fleeces from the summer shearing of hundreds of sheep may not have been enough to supply the clothmakers of Mirfield and the nearby villages, and so Adam de Hopton, like his father before him, was dealing in wool. His father, also Adam de Hopton, was certainly dealing in wool in 1307 when he purchased 'one sack of wool, good, clean and saleable worth £10', from a merchant of York to whom he was pledged for repayment of the debt. Later that year a debt was registered for £4 10s. and half a sack of wool owing to the same merchant (a sack was 364 lbs). It seems that the Hoptons were middle men supplying wool to cloth-makers.

Just how cloth-making was organized locally at this time is not known, or how many people in the township were involved in one way or another. There may have been men buying wool and working independently to produce a piece of cloth but by the early fourteenth century there may also have also been men, possibly Adam de Hopton himself, who employed workers who were paid to prepare and spin the wool and weave the 'pieces' and they themselves selling the finished cloth.

The process of making woollen cloth began with sorting the wool of a fleece according to the quality of fibre and then removing adhering dirt before washing and greasing it and making it ready for spinning. The wool purchased by Adam de Hopton had already gone through some of these processes. Later evidence shows that washing wool could be outdoor work, sometimes done in the nearest stream or well (spring). At much later manor courts in 1628 and 1629 it was ordered that wool should not be washed in the Town Brook or the well at Wellhouse on penalty of a fine of 3 shillings and 4 pence, as these were sources of water for the nearby households. The cleaned wool was then dried, greased and the fibres teased out to loosen them ready for spinning into yarn. Up to this point children might help with some of the work as few went to school and learned to work from a young age. Spinning the wool to make yarn was mostly done by the women, both rich and poor, and a distaff, a spindle with a weight, and eventually spinning wheel, was just as likely to to be found in the manor houses as well as the cottages. There was always a steady demand for yarn to supply the weavers and unmarried women often supported themselves in this way, these were the 'spinsters'. It was often the men who set up the horizontal wooden looms and wove the 'pieces'.

The loosely woven pieces from the looms were converted into useable cloth at the fulling mill, where mechanization had replaced the work formerly done by the 'walker'. The preliminary scouring to remove any grease was done by using a detergent of stale urine and lye (potash, extracted from boiling woodash) or alternatively fullers earth. It was said that fullers could be recognized by their smell. The wet cloth was then placed in a wooden trough where it could be pounded with heavy wooden mallets or stocks powered by a water wheel. Before this mechanization this matting of the fibres together which resulted in shrinking the cloth was formerly done by the 'walker', who trampled the wet cloth with his feet. Finally the cloth was taken out to the tenter garth or ground and attached by metal hooks to the wooden tenter frames and stretched to dry to a standard size. Before the cloth could br taken from the mill the fuller must attach a small lead seal to each 'piece' to verify that the cloth was of a statute width and that the prescribed tax levied on a piece of cloth had been paid, and of course the fuller for his work and his 'soap'.

Things did not always go smoothly though, and a badly worn fragment of a court roll for the de Heton manor in 1367 records a dispute at what must have been the West Mill when the fuller, Richard Walker, brought a plea of debt against William Scot for work done on his cloth and for soap. William Scot charged the fuller with breaking his agreement for the work which was to be done on his cloth at Richard's fulling mill and that the work was not done within the agreed time. Presumably impatient to have his cloth William had broken the fence of the tenter garth and taken it away without paying the fuller. Unfortunately there is no surviving court roll to tell how this dispute was resolved.

Nicholas the fuller who witnessed a deed of conveyance in 1326 was also mentioned as Nicholas le Walker in 1332 and another fuller named John is mentioned in 1331. Walker continued as a surname, but others asscociated with cloth making such as litster (Lister) a dyer, or weaver (Webster) have not been found in medieval Mirfield, although there certainly was a litster in Dewsbury. Dying cloth was a skilled occupation and much of the cloth made in Mirfield may have been left a natural drab colour, although some yarn might be dyed before weaving (dyed in the wool) as part of the domestic process. If there were a number of weavers then Webster as a descriptive name may have been of little use.

Difficult Times

The weather in the years 1314, 1315 and 1316 was dreadful, with almost continuous rain. Everywhere it was reported that the seed sown in waterlogged fields did not germinate and poor harvests were ruined. Here any water banks would be overwhelmed and the cultivated strips in the Netherholme and other land near the river must have been flooded. The Broadsike, swollen with the water draining from the sodden land, probably overflowed and much of the lower Eastfield would be waterlogged. There would be damp walls, leaking thatch, muddy tracks, sticky soil and sodden clothes; all this must have been endured during these miserable years. Inevitably, there would be a scarcity of corn and the price of grain soared; some might eat their seed corn and sell their plough oxen to find money for food. Misfortune continued in the next few years with widespread outbreaks of murrain, a disease which caused death amongst the sheep and cattle. This was a time of widespread famine when, it has been suggested, malnutrition was responsible for a general fall in population of between 10 to 15% between the years 1315 and 1320. There is no way of knowing what disasters were experienced in Mirfield township, or how well or badly the inhabitants fared. In the very wet years of the early fourteenth century flooding was probably severe, creating what Ismay described after a flood in the eighteenth century, as a scene of devastation, with the fields strewn with boulders and debris, and the crops ruined.

Added to all this the war in Scotland continued and Scots raided into England as far south as Yorkshire after 1314. If there was not immediate danger there was anxiety. Some years later the the Prior of Nostell, whose priory was by then in financial straights, claimed to have suffered many misfortunes. Among them was income lost through Scots incursions, which included profits from Birstall, Morley, Batley and Rothwell and the priory being plundered and horses taken by the king's master of horse before Boroughbridge (1322), and then murrain, so they had no oxen or cows to plough with.

It was at the battle at Boroughbridge that a royalist force supporting Edward II met and defeated that of the rebels under Henry, Earl of Lancaster and lord of the Honour of Pontefract. News would not be long arriving of the defeat, of the Earl's execution at Pontefract, and then the hanging of rebels, some in their own villages, and possibly local men may have been implicated. Adam de Everingham, who had a holding of a carucate in Mirfield, was lucky to escape with his life after imprisonment and a huge fine.

At the beginning of the fourteenth century the population had probably reached its peak of about two hundred or so people. By 1320 there may have been fewer, possibly there had been more deaths than usual, especially among the poorer tenants, people debilitated by malnutrition. There may also have been a few empty cottages. With some improvement in the weather, however, the field land that had been temporarily abandoned when flooded or waterlogged, was worked again. Pastures that had been almost empty after the murrain would be gradually re-stocked. For a time during the late 1320s the weather, though unpredictable, was warmer, but sometimes there were droughts before more wet years and poor harvests. In 1331 there were floods and at Wakefield the fulling mill was ' broken and defective on account of the rising river' and both it and the corn mill stood idle for several months (Wakefield Court Rolls).

Whatever had happened in Mirfield during those bad years of the early fourteenth century, the usual pattern of life in the township continued. John de Heton, son of Sir John de Heton, had died about 1307, only about four years after his father and Thomas, his brother, was now lord of the manor of Castle. The new rector, William de Soothill, a canon of Beverly Minster who had succeeded John de Heton, resigned in 1317 and was replaced by William de Cressacre, who was instituted on the 4th.of May 1318.

An exchange of land in 1319 affords a tantalizing glimpse of one part of the township. William the smith of Mirfield (already mentioned) exchanged a perch of his land in the fields of Mirfield, bought from William son of Sabine, for one more conveniently near his premises. In exchange for the perch, which lay between 'the land held by Richard the chaplain and the selion held by Adam del Leigh [held]from Thomas de Heton', John de Pontefract granted him a strip of land 'lying between the land of Thomas de Heton on either side, the house of Emma daughter of Margery and abutting on the one end on the brook running by the said William's forge'. The only part of Mirfield that might fit this description was on the western side of the township, in the field land known as Ratten Rawe. That could be between the few houses of the hamlet, near the highway, and the stream forming the north-western boundary of the township and nearby was Cinder Hills, a possible site of iron smelting.

There are a few more documents from the first part of the fourteenth century, all being deeds relating to the transference of property. These contain names of people, but provide little other information about the township. In 1326 Thomas de Heton died and his son John finally released to Geoffrey the baker the toft with a messuage that he had held as a freehold in his father's manor. The same year, William the smith secured the inheritance of his property, which included his forge, to his daughter Joan, who had married Adam de Helay, and in 1332 she granted the same to her son Richard. Another daughter who inheritsd at this time was Avicia daughter of Thomas de Hopton, who in 1334 was to have her father's lands and all his goods 'moveable and unmoveable'. This left nothing for his widow apart from the lands settled on her as dower, when she eventually remarried she granted her dower lands to Avicia who was by then married John le Taylor. The witnesses who were called upon to add their names to these deeds were often landholders or relatives who might be affected by the transaction. Those who appear regularly were the well recorded Adam de Hopton, Adam de Helay, William by the Water, Richard de Northorpe, William de Mirfield and then for some reason Nicholas the fuller (twice) and on one occasion, Richard the cowherd.

John de Pontefract of Mirfield, mentioned in 1326, was the last of the de Pontefract name in Mirfield. and later their lands appear to have belonged to the de Mirfields.

Possibly this came by the marriage with a daughter and heir of John de Pontefract, or possibly by purchase. The de Mirfields held a manor in Mirfield until the sixteenth century, when, after the death of William de Mirfield of Howley, it passed to Thomas Wentworth. of Goxhill, Lincolnshire.

When Thomas de Heton died in 1326 the inquisition into his lands recorded that 'Thomas de Heton has a messuage and one and a half bovates [possibly carucates] in Mirfield held of the king in chief by knight service … doing service of the king's court at Pontefract. John, the next heir is aged 30 yrs'. Five years later, on the 7th of November 1331, this John de Heton, then aged about 35 years and probably sick, made provision for his two sons, William and Thomas. He granted them rents in Mirfield and Hopton, but secured the reversion (in the event of their deaths) to himself and then to John his heir and the heirs by Agnes de Methley his wife. John died before the 15th of December when Alice (also referred to as Agnes), former wife (widow) of John de Heton claimed to have had joint tenancy in East or Earlsheaton (Wakefield Court Rolls). The next John de Heton, his heir, was then about seven years old. Nothing more is known of Thomas de Heton but William enters the story again later.

CHAPTER ELEVEN

The Black Death
and a case of insanity

A Virulent Disease

In June 1348, in the hot summer, the Black Death struck the south-west of England. It was highly contagious, usually fatal, and the true cause was not known. The disease spread rapidly and the number of deaths was enormous, though no one counted them. In July 1348 the Archbishop of York ordered penitential processions to be made in all churches on Wednesdays and Fridays, during which prayers were to be said and the litany of the saints recited to avert the plague. In late 1348 the contagion may have reached the western side of Yorkshire and although the winter of 1348/9 was bitterly cold the disease continued to spread. No one wrote about it, but at the court for the Manor of Wakefield, held at Brighouse in late 1348, a much higher than usual number of heriots (a death duty) were paid. In the summer of 1349 many more people than usual were taking up land previously occupied by relatives or others in that manor. Nothing is known of what happened in Mirfield, but the fear and panic can be imagined as people learned of the rapid onset of the disease and the almost certain death that followed.

If the Black Death reached Mirfield, and it seems unlikely that it did not, then the death toll must have been high. It is thought that one third to a half of the population of England died of the pestilence, though in some places the mortality was greater than in others. In the archdiocese of York a third of the clergy, whose duty it was to visit the sick, are known to have died. Nearby at Kirklees the prioress was one of the prioresses that the Archbishop listed as having died. Fearful and trying to avoid contagion, there would be a reluctance to help sick neighbours and the dead would be buried with haste. Where families had succumbed there would be empty cottages, neglected farmyards and land lying uncultivated in the fields.

By 1350 the epidemic was waning, but the survivors faced a very wet year. The accounts for the Rectory Manor of Dewsbury show payments made for digging ditches to keep the water (from the river) out of the churchyard. Once again the lower parts of Mirfield's East Field and the Netherholme would be waterlogged or flooded. The same accounts for Dewsbury also show that the money received from the sale of tithe corn collected from Middlestown, Flockton and the chapelry of Hartshead for the year from Michaelmas (end of September) 1349 to Michaelmas 1350 was less than half that collected the year before and there was nothing from Brighouse. In the Manor of Wakefield there were lands said to have been 'in decay' for a year 'without tenants'. It is hard to believe that Mirfield township had escaped the Black Death and was flourishing. At Castle Hall things were certainly not going well.

The Madness of John de Heton

On 25th of July 1348, as news of the dreadful contagion was spreading, John de Heton of Castle Hall was said to have lost his wits and from that time had been insane; he was twenty four years old. He and his wife Margaret had three young children, John the eldest then William and Joan. John, who may have been about six years old, was already married, or soon to be married to, Margery daughter of Adam de Hopton. She was to be part of the household at Castle Hall. Her age is not known, possibly she was in her teens otherwise she would, as was usual, though married, have been still with he parents. Also at Castle Hall was William de Heton, John's brother, a clergyman, and there would be the household servants.

More than six years was to elapse before, on a cold day in early January 1355, John de Heaton was taken to Doncaster where William de Fynchenden and John de Upton were to enquire and certify whether he was an idiot. In answer to their questions it was said that 'up to that time [24th of July 1348] he was in good sense and quite sane and ... since then until today he has been continuously an idiot, insensible to his surroundings having a fancy in his head whereby he remains unconscious of his own personality and paying no heed to anything at all. He enjoys no lucid intervals.'

From the inquiry at Doncaster comes the barest outline of the what must have been fraught times at Castle Hall during those years. It was said that John's wife, Margaret, had been managing the household and her sick husband until, after four years, she had refused to live any longer in the same house with William. What role her brother in law William de Heton played is not known, but trouble there was and Margaret claimed 'he would not let her have charge of her husband'. At the end of September 1352 the family was split, Margaret and her son John and his wife Margery going to live in Adam de Hopton's household. William was left with the care of his sick brother and the two younger children and the family assets were divided between the two parties.

John de Heton had been born on the 25th March 1324, son of John de Heton and his wife Agnes. His father died on December 1331 when John was short of eight years old. This was a family of minor gentry and not wealthy. Their income from rents was £9 15s 10d a year and what accrued from the demesne of the manor of Castle in Mirfield; together this put them below the £20 income required of a knight. A marriage was probably arranged for John when he was about seventeen years old but the age of his wife Margaret is not known; she may have been older. Their first son, John, was born about 1344 when John was eighteen years of age and there were two other known children in the next four years, William and Joan. It was a young household at Castle Hall in 1348 when disaster struck.

William de Heton, John's brother, must have been at least in 'minor orders' of the clergy, if not a priest, when John had failed to present him to the rectory of Mirfield in 1347. He never seems to have married. There may have been several reasons for the quarrel that had led to Margaret's departure and Adam de Hopton may have had some part in the matter. He had probably instigated the marriage of his daughter to the young John, not long after John de Heton came of age and so had control of his own affairs. In the event he certainly got control of his young son in law, the heir to the de Heton lands.

Adam de Hopton seems to have been determined to further the fortunes of his family, and John de Heton may have been easily manipulated. Adam had appeared before the ecclesiastical court at York accused in a case of forced marriage, having compelled his son William, aged nine years, to marry an unwilling bride who was about twenty years old and who claimed she had been already secretly married. The bride, though nearly of age, was still Adam's ward and he had control of her lands. The pair had been forceable brought to the altar weeping and under threat of violence.

It was Adam de Hopon who had caused the writ to be issued ordering a full enquiry to be made into the matter of John de Heton's idiocy and also claiming the inadequacy of Margaret's income. The de Heton holding in Mirfield was said to be a messuage with 140 acres of demesne, and five acres of meadow. There was also a mill and 37 shillings rents from free tenants. The chattels (animals) belonging were 6 oxen, 4 horses and 40 sheep, presumably used on the demesne farm (the household goods are not mentioned). The rest of the properties were smaller manors in Kirkheaton (West Heaton) and Earlsheaton (East Heaton) and rents from lands in East Ardsley and Pollington in Balne. Margaret had been allowed the income from Earlsheaton and East Ardsley and her half of the goods and chattels. Unfortunately, all the sheep had died of the murrain in the winter of 1352 and Adam de Hopton claimed there was not enough income to keep Margaret and her son and his wife.

It the event it was decided that the goods and chattels, as apportioned, were to remain (as already agreed) between William and Margaret, John's wife. Also that

William de Heton, John de Malet, who had married John's aunt, and John de Helay his brother-in-law, 'were nearest relations and friends of the said John and can best have the guardianship of him'. On the 18th March the matter was closed when 'it has been found by inquisition that John de Heton after completing his twenty fourth year has become an idiot, the king has committed to John Malet, John Shellay and William de Heton the keeping of the body and the lands of the said John' (Patent Rolls). John de Shellay was also an uncle by marriage, having married Anne de Heton.

John de Heton was forty eight years old when he died in 1372. What exactly he suffered from for half of his life and how he was treated we will never know. His son John, already thirty or more years old when his father died, paid the relief to take up the inheritance. The last of the de Heton name to hold that 'third of Mirfield known as the manor of Chastell'.

CHAPTER TWELVE

A Manor Court and the Poll Tax
1350 to 1400

All those named in the inquisition into the idiocy of John de Heton had certainly survived any outbreak of plague in 1349. Adam de Hopton, merchant and landholder, continued to prosper. He had married the heiress to the manor of Armley and was to make Armley Hall his home. He also had married his children advantageously into the local 'gentry' families. He was now wealthy and able to lend large sums of money; one loan of £100 was to John Beaumont of Crossland (to whom he was now related by marriage). He never achieved gentry status and was described as 'franklin', a wealthy freeholder, in the poll tax for Armley in 1379. His will made on 7th of January 1384 was brief and unusual. His wish was to be buried at St Peter's church Leeds and he left:

> 10 shillings to see me buried honourably. To the roofing of Leeds Parish church 6s 8d. And for the damage done by my animals, whatsoever, in the parishes of Mirfield, Hopton, Thornhill and Dewsbury 14s. To a certain servant who I badly beat 2s. For satisfaction for a colt which was injured in Thornhill Park 54 shillings and for many times hunting with my dogs.

There were no other beneficiaries mentioned, nor bequest to the church at Mirfield, the parish where he had spent much of his life. A man capable, violent and ruthless and probably of no good reputation he had lived to the very old age for those days of eighty years.

Another survivor was William de Mirfield, lawyer, now Sir William, a Justice of the Peace, and who amongst his many offices was to be a collector of the Poll Tax in the West Riding and also a deputy sheriff of the county and was now probably the largest landholder in Mirfield.

There were outbreaks of the plague in 1361 and 1369, which possibly affected the township, that of 1361 especially taking toll among children, and there were to be more outbreaks in the following century, any of which may have reached Mirfield. There is nothing known of these times when whole families could be wiped out, children orphaned and parents who lost children. In a community where land and live stock had to be tended there may have been fewer hands for the work. It was a time when some tenants might benefit by taking land left vacant and so increased their holdings and some be able to take land for the first time.

On the Tuesday before the feast of St. Thomas (21st of December) 1366 a manor court was held by John de Shelley, steward for John de Heton. A small and damaged fragment written in latin records some of the proceedings at that court. Unfortunately, the list of tenants such as that found in later rolls is missing. The surviving section is mostly taken up with the claims and counter claims made by Richard le Walker, the fuller, [at West Mill] and William Scot in a dispute concerning the fulling of cloth at the fulling mill, a dispute that has already been mentioned (see above).

There is, however, the first reference to coal mining in Mirfield when Thomas de Northorpe and Robert del Stokkes, were ordered 'that they remove, before the next court, all that soil and clay that they had put onto the lord's land [when] digging and searching for coal'. The digging had presumably be done on the common land, since the commons belonged to the manor lord and so did the coal beneath them. Coal was another asset belonging to the manor and licence to dig had to be obtained. Presumably, Thomas and Robert had a licence but had not filled in the pits, an offence that was also recorded at a later court. Although this is the first reference to digging coal in Mirfield it was almost certainly something that was happening long before that date. Thomas and Robert both had land in and near Northorpe and a later enclosed piece of land at the lower end of Shillbank, between Crossley Lane and Shillbank Lane, was named Pit Ing. Thomas del Northorpe, merchant, appears in the list of inhabitants who paid poll tax thirteen years later in 1379, possibly the same person. If so it would seem unlikely that he himself had dug for the coal.

Shortly after holding this court John de Shelley who had presided at the court, and William de Mirfield, were to set out on a pilgrimage 'beyond the seas'. To do this they had obtained licence from the king to be absent from the kingdom for a year. It would be a long, hazardous and expensive journey, possibly they intended to visit the Holy Land and possibly, like many others, they made their wills before they set out. In the event they came safely home, at least William de Mirfield did if he was the same who appears below.

In 1379 the collector for the Poll Tax made a list of all who paid the tax in the parish of Mirfield (which included Hopton). All over 16 years of age were to pay and a husband and wife were assessed together. It was a graduated tax starting with a basic rate of 4 pence. Heading the list was Sir William himself who paid 20 shillings. He was the wealthiest inhabitant by far and had six servants who each paid 4 pence. The others who paid more than the basic 4 pence were John de Boulton, franklin (yeoman freeholder) who paid 3 shillings and 4 pence, and Robert del Stones and Thomas de Northorpe, both merchants who each paid twelve pence. There were also the four craftsmen who paid 6 pence, two tailors, Thomas Beche and Thomas Ridilsden and Adam Fox, carpenter and John Benet, shoemaker. Twenty other men, with there wives, paid the basic 4 pence, but only the men are named. There were also thirty eight others over 16 years of age also who paid 4 pence. John de Heton and his household have not been found in the surviving returns for any of their properties, but evasions were not uncommon.

The list allows the following estimation to be made of the size of the population of Mirfield with Hopton in 1379. The 28 married couples each represent a household and there were 44 others above 16 years of age. Of these 19 were either identified as servants or those whose names suggest that they were part of the family in one or other of the households. The remaining 15 others may have lived independently. A calculation allowing 4.5 perons per household and adding the 15 others single or independent and 6 servants would give a population of about 130. Allowing five persons on average per household, there might have been about 150 persons. This estimate of number would suggest a population of less than the 200 suggested for the beginning of the fourteenth century. From these rough calculations it seems possible that the population had shrunk by at least a quarter or almost a third though, whether as a result of an outbreak of plague is not known.

It is probable that there was little increase in the number of people living in the township until the end of the fifteenth century. The expectation of life is thought to have fallen by about 10 years by the late fourteenth century making it the period of lowest life expectancy in medieval times.

There had been further decades when the weather was predominantly wet as in the 1360s, and others when there was drought and poor harvests. By the later part of the fourteenth century some of the less productive arable field land in the township had probably been returned to pasture, a change that was widespread at that time. There may have been vacant tofts where cottages and buildings had not long survived being empty and so neglected; probably the valuable and useable timber having been taken away. Although it is difficult to make monetary comparisons the mill belonging to the manor of Castle, which had been valued at £10 13s 4d a year in 1249, was let for far less in 1391. On the 4th of November of that year 'John de Heton of Mirfield leased to Richard Walker of same his watermill and fulling mill in the township of Mirfield and a plot of land and meadow lying between the Helme on the south side and the water of Keldyr on the north from Martinmas (11th November) for a term of 30 years at a yearly rent of 30s [£1 10s] payable at Whitsuntide and Martinmas'. John de Heton was 'to find the mill stones and timber for the repair and building of the mills. Walker to find the iron and other necessary articles and to hand over the mill in good condition at the end of the term'. The witness to the transaction was Robert Stokkes of Mirfield. Walker had become a surname for tenants of the mill and a William Walker appears in the Poll Tax list. Possibly Robert Stokkes was the same, who when mentioned in the court roll of 1367, had been a much younger man, who had been digging for coal. He would certainly be the Robert del Stokkes, the parishioner who in 1399 was nominated to assist in caring for the aging, last rector, John Wylgyn. The 'aged and feeble' rector died soon after in 1400 by which time the rectory of Mirfield had been conveyed to the Prioress and Convent of Kirklees. There was soon to be a small house in Towngate for a vicar and which later, in the eighteenth century, became the kitchen for Joseph Ismay's parsonage, now Ivy Lodge.

The few surviving documents from this time give no hint of any of the floods, famine, disease, war, rebellion and political uproar that occurred in the fourteenth century. These must have been times of danger and frought with anxiety for the people in the township. As this century was coming to an end such was the unrest that in September 1398 Archbishop Scrope of York ordered that all parishioners were to make penitential processions round their churches and that prayers were to be said 'for the deliverance of the king, the people and the Church from pestilence and other miseries'. Richard II, blamed for the hated poll taxes, was deposed and then taken and imprisoned in the castle at Pontefract. In the bleak weather in February 1400 would come the news that the king was dead; rumour was that he had died of starvation. The poet, John Gower, wrote of the world 'that it was well nigh turned upside down' (Whitock).

The Poll Tax Return of 1379

William de Mirfield, knight, and wife	20s. 0d.
John de Boulton, franklin, and wife	3s. 4d.
Robert de Stones, merchant, and wife	12d.
Thomas del Northorp, merchant, and wife	12d.
Thomas Beche, tailor, and wife	6d.
Adam Fox, carpenter, and wife	6d.
Thomas Ridilsden, tailor, and wife	6d.
John Benet, shoenmaker, and wife	6d.

All those below paid 4d.

Richard Mersland and wife
Roger Milner and wife
William Walker and wife
John de Denby and wife
Adam Ascy and wife
John de Stokes and wife
Thomas Pynder and wife
John Pynder and wife
William del Cote and wife
Richard Smyth and wife
Adam Waller and wife
Hugh Broune and wife
John Ascy and wife
William Gyffon and wife
Richard Tomson and wife
Adam son of Henry and wife
John Primerose and wife
Richard de ffournays and wife
John be the water and wife
Johnde Helay and wife
John servant of William Mirfield
William servant of the same
Robert servant of the same
Adam servant of the same
Isabell servant of the same
Emma servant of the same
John Buktrowte

Margaret Denby
John Tude
William Taliour
Amice Taliour
Juliana daughter of Amice
Joan Smyth
Thomas Smyth
Alice del Legh
John del Legh
Juliana Waller
Katerine Waller
Isabell Helmanden
John servant of Isabell
William Gutell
Elizabeth Pynder
Robert servant of Robert
Henry servant of John
John de Batelay
Joan Northorp
Alice Benet
Juliana de Heton
Margaret de Heton
Amabil servant of Roger
Joan de Alberter
John atte Water
John de Northorp
Joan de Northorp
John Wilkinson
Agnes daughter of Robert
Emma daughter of Robert
Isabell daughter of Walter
John Nelson
William Hobman
Robert de Esthagh
Adam Watson
Isabell Watdoghter
Agnes de Northorp

CHAPTER THIRTEEN

Late Medieval Mirfield

O n the Tuesday next after the feast of St Luke the Evangelist, the sixth year of king Henry the sixth (October 1427), William de Mirfield held a manor court at Mirfield. He was living at Howley Hall in Batley parish and by now his manor courts here were probably only being held twice a year. The few damaged pieces of parchment that have survived as a record of several of these courts give the names of William de Mirfield's tenants and record a few instances of infringements of the manor bye laws, orders given for work to be done and changes of tenancy. At the court held in October 1427 the names of the six tenants who were sworn as the panel or jury were Thomas Walker, John Gascoigne, John Ffournes, Thomas, Northorpe, John by the water and, unusually a woman tenant, Mary Fox. They presented that 'Henry de Dewsbury and Thomas Couper, had grazed the pastures of Mirfield with all their oxen to the damage of the lord and a tenant Richard Liversedge [had done] the same with a horse on Mirfield Moor and he has therefore fled.' This was a serious offence, as the common pasture was essential grazing for the livestock in the township. The only other matter recorded was the order that 'for any pigs that were not ringed before the feast of the Nativity (Christmas) next, for each two [pigs] 12 pence (fine)'. This last was common practice as putting a ring through the noses of pigs prevented them routling up the ground at times when they were allowed to forage on the commons and in the woods.

The twenty tenants who should attend the court held six years later on the 12th of October in the 12th year of Henry the sixth (1433) were named as Robert Hopton, John by the water, John Ffournes, Richard Northorpe and Mary his wife, for land formerly Adam Fox, Thomas Walker, Thomas Northorpe's heir, William Taylor, John Legh, Richard Legh, Richard Grenegate, John Byrton, Richard Byrton, John Jepson, John Legh, junior, John Jepson, Henry Mabinsell, Thomas Legh, John Abey and John Fletcher. Nothing else was recorded for this court although from it can be deduced that Thomas Northorpe had died and Richard Northorpe, presumably Thomas' son and heir, had inherited his father's holding. Richard was then in a position to marry and had married Mary Fox. She was a tenant holding land in her own right and so he was now farming more land. Mary was probably the daughter and heir of Adam Fox and granddaughter of Adam Fox the carpenter who paid Poll Tax in 1379. As she was a tenant in her own right at the time of the court held in 1427, she may have been at least in her twenties when she married and seems to have been the last of the Fox name in medieval Mirfield.

At a court held four years later on the 25th of March 1437 there was only a very small panel of four sworn, these being Richard Legh, Robert at Legh, John at the Grenegate and Richard Northorpe. It was said that 'Thomas Legh should repair the barn at the Overhall before Easter' and the tenant who stood pledged to see that this was done was William Legh; who he himself would be fined if the work was not done. Then William Broke (Brook) and [others] said that John Broke of Feldhouse carried away several (planks) of the lord's wood and that Richard Burton bought the same wood for two shillings'. There was also a change of tenant registered when Robert Legh 'came to this court and took all that land and tenement that were formerly [belonging to] Richard Grenegate.' There were also orders made for the cutting of hay and keeping sheep on the meadow, after the hay was taken, and fences to be made, as well as for cutting the corn. Since the court was held in March, these were things that would only be done later in the summer but before the next court.

The impression gained from these surviving scraps of information, the small numbers of tenants forming the panels, and the lack of business all point to it being a far from a thriving manor at that time. The customary courts had to beheld but apparently not all tenants attended and the profits were small. These were not times when people were prospering, the summers being poor and the winters very cold. Harvests were often meagre and some villages were shrinking while others were abandoned. There were further outbreaks of plague in some places and in Mirfield, as elsewhere, there was probably little increase in the number of people in the township .

In the common fields land was still being cultivated in individual strips, although the move to consolidate them into more compact blocks went on. Exchanges to achieve this were not just made for convenience of working, but so that the land could be enclosed with hedges and used as the tenant wished. This was a move favoured by those tenants with fairly large holdings, like Richard Northorpe, who would see opportunity in using their enclosed land for whatever was most profitable. Soon these closes of land would be described as being arable, meadow or pasture. In 1405/6 two of the largest landholders Robert de Hopton, son and heir of Adam de Hopton, and John de Heton made an exchange of land which illustrates the process by which the landscape was changing. Robert agreed to release two and a half acres in the Netherholme to

John de Heton in exchange for three and a half acres of land in a 'furlong called Rattenrawe' and in another place called 'Whitlegh'. The land in the Netherholme that was transferred to John de Heton was adjacent to land that he had already enclosed. The land at Rattunrawe and nearby Whitlegh having been won by the clearance of Mirfield Wood was probably less productive and better used as pasture than that on the fertile alluvial soil of the Netherholme. This may account for a bigger acreage transfered to Robert de Hopton. The patchwork of small fields, hedged enclosures or closes that Ismay described was now emerging.

For much of the fifteenth century the civil war between the houses of York and Lancaster - the Wars of the Roses - must have had an impact on ordinary peoples near the places where battles and skirmishes took place. When there were battles that involved the greater landholders support was demanded from their lesser tenants. In 1460 the conflict came close to Mirfield when the Duke of York reached his castle at Sandal, near Wakefield, on the 21st of December. Sir John Savile of Thornhill was then constable of the castle and a supporter of the Yorkist faction. It was a wet, cold and tense Christmastide. The Yorkists were at Sandal and the Lancastrians were in force at Pontefract Castle. On the 30th of December came the clash between the two opposing sides in the fields below the castle at Sandal, the Duke of York and his eldest son being killed as they fled to Wakefield. Sir Johnn Savile had no doubt rallied his tenants and many others who may have been at Wakefield. Three months later on the 29th March the battle of Towton was fought in a late snowstorm, with terrible loss of life. Some in the township who may have rallied to support one side or the other may have been amongst the 60,000 men who are said to have fought there and been among the many who were maimed or killed. News of these disasters came by word of mouth and nothing was set down to tell of what was happening in the lives of the ordinary people here or elsewhere.

All this was in the past when a court for the Manor of Castle was held for the Gascoignes in July 1475. The de Hetons had continued at Castle Hall until sometime after 1427, when their tenure of the manor ended with the death of the last John de Heton. Isabel de Heton, daughter of William de Heton and heir of her uncle, John de Heton, had married John Gascoigne of Lasingcroft and the Gascoignes had become lords of the manor. They were absentee lords and Castle Hall was occupied by a tenant one eventually being John Soothill, a younger son John Soothill of Soothill.

The surviving record of the court held in July 1475 is very badly damaged, but the names of the freehold tenants were William Mirfield, Robert Hopton for Geoffrey Backster land, Mary Fox land and Cliderocote, John Soothill, junior; for William [Graneson] land, William Issot, John Netilton, Richard Legh's heirs, John Northorpe, Thomas Walker, Robert Ffournes, John [Gibson] Richard Thurgoland heirs, John

Dighton, Thomas Rodes of Flockton. Nine people were fined for cutting and carrying away wood. Edward Lee, William Hall, John Lee, William Netilton, William Isott, Thomas Armitage , Elizabeth Northorpe, Mary Jepson, John Crowder. There was also an order concerning 'any who had searched and dug for coal and not filling the pits to be fined 4 pence for any pit'; the rest is illegible.

Some of those named had land in both manors and some, like Robert Hopton of Armley, had a number of sub-tenants in Mirfield. One of his properties was the messuage later named as Blake Hall, but still known as Geoffrey Bakster land then even though a century had passed since Geoffrey had first taken possession of it. The name Blake Hall is first encountered in the parish registers in 1569 and in the 1570s was occupied by Christopher Hopton who may have rebuilt it (Ismay). John Soothill, junior, was the tenant of Castle Hall and its demesne lands and his daughter was to marry John Beaumont. On the 20th June 1484 a covenant was made between John Soothill the younger, esq. and John Beaumont, gent., that John Beaumont, John Beaumont's son and heir shall marry Alice, daughter of John Soothill the younger, esq. [her] fortune £30'. From the time when John and Alice went to live at Castle Hall the Beaomonts were established there. Although they purchased the estate 'known by the name of the Manor of Mirfield or Chastel', they were never lords of that manor.

Court rolls, as they were known, were made up of sheets of parchment, sometimes scraped clean of writing and reused, on which were recorded the business of a court. Consecutive sheets were stitched foot to top in a way that they formed a strip that was rolled up for storage. Until the seventeenth century these were written in latin. The only full sheet from medieval times is the record of a court held in January 1485 by Sir William Mirfield. This provides the most complete and informative survival of all the medieval court records for Mirfield. There were now thirty tenants who were named as the panel: Richard Legh, Robert Legh, John Bayly, James Hermitage (Armitage), Richard Burton, Thomas Burton, William Legh, Thomas Legh, Richard Jepson , Henry Yle, Perceval by the Broke, William Syke, Thomas by the Broke, Thomas Stede, John Scot, John Tyler (? Taylor), Anthony Mabinsell, Thomas Hermitage, Thomas Walker, William Netilton, John Barker, Robert Barker, John Gledhill, Robert Ashton, John Walker, Richard Mabinsell, John by the Broke, John Ffournes, Robert of ye Nuke (Nook). John Legh of Hopton. Other tenants who it was said should have attended the court but had not come were. Robert Whitley's heirs, John Water, William Couper and John Hurst of Gledhill. Some of these were probably from his holdings other than in Mirfield.

There was always the problem of obtaining wood and fines for taking wood without permission appear on most court rolls. The small trees, branches, shrubs, and even ivy and other greenery that could be used as fuel for a fire, for making fencing or as fodder for animals were in demand. There may have been the right to collect dead wood but cutting and taking all types of wood without permission was prohibited although it was a common offence reported at most courts. At this court there was the warning given that 'anyone taking away neither green trees nor any other the lord's wood, nor thorns growing on the moor or boughs, fine 4 pence for any of these offences'. That fine could amount to two days wages for some people but despite any previous order Richard Lee, William Netilton and William Issot had taken 'green wood from the lord's commons for their own use and Thomas Armitage, Elizabeth Northorpe and John Crowther had cut down and taken wood'; all were fined.

Trees, especially those being managed in the lord's woods, were valuable since they were the source of timber for building, of poles from the coppices and bark for the tanning of leather. The wood yard where the timber was dealt with was probably at its busiest after trees had been felled in autumn and were brought in to be sawn and worked while still green, before it hardened. It was therefore ordered that 'no one was to obstruct the sawpitte before the 6th of January (Holy Innocents Day) on pain of a fine of 11d. What might happen to obstruct the saw pit is not mentioned. This was a serious offence and suggests an urgency in working the timber, most of which probably came from woods in Hopton, so that it would eventually be sold.

Other autumn work for the tenants would have been the sowing of winter wheat in parts of the common fields. The crops then had to be protected from the animals that might stray from their grazing on the adjacent commons.and so it was ordered that 'anyone not sufficiently making their doles (their length of the wattle fences) round the sown fields before November 30th [St. Andrew's Day], or round the fallow field before 25th March to be fined 4 pence for every dole[not made]'. Livestock were put to graze the stubble and weeds on the land to be left fallow or uncultivated that year their dung adding to the fertilirty of he soil.

Winter ploughing would be followed by the sowing of the spring corn, usually barley and oats. Despite any steps taken to prevent, it livestock could stray onto growing crops and cause damage by trampling and grazing. The pinder would impound any strays, but their owners were often reluctant to pay for the fine for their release. 'Breaking the common fold' and 'rescuing' animals without paying the fine was a common offence and therefore it was said at this court that for 'breaking the lord's common pinfold' there was a fine of 4d.

Rents were a large part of the income from the manor and taking, and enclosing a piece of land without permission and so avoiding paying rent for it was an offence. The amounts of land taken in by the tenants were often quite small and sometimes achieved by moving a fence or hedge. John Legh who had 'taken a piece from the lord's waste at Westmylle' was ordered to pay 12d before the next court. He was probably allowed to keep the land and pay rent. At courts in the seventeenth century such 'encroachments were ordered to be 'thrown open' again. Everything on the manor was an asset that had to be protected, and tenants seem to have been responsible for the maintainance of all the buildings they occupied. It was ordered that tenants repair the buildings on their tenements before St Martin's Day (the 11th of November) or face a fine of 6s 8d (half a mark, or 80d). That was an enormous fine and was intended to make sure the properties were in good repair before the winter set in.

Finally, as at another court, came the order that anyone who had dug pits 'searching and digging for coal' should fill them or face a fine of 4d for every pit not filled. This suggests that there were more than a few such diggings for coal and that the unfilled pits were a danger to people and animals. Here at least was an order which, if for no other reason, would benefit the inhabitants.

The money paid in fines at the court belonged Sir William Mirfield, and the amounts were by no means small although they appear so today. A skilled craftsman such as a carpenter might be paid as much as 4d a day, others for heavy work such as ploughing and reaping 2d and 1 penny for other light work. Those people who had little or no land were dependent on wages. There were no fixed incomes as in recent times. Work was rarely regular and wages were paid by the day. No work was done on Sundays and other Holy Days (holidays) - the important Feast days of the Church. In addition, there were also quite a number of saints days, not to mention the twelve days of Christmas. Work on the land was seasonal, and ploughing, hay time and harvest demanded plenty of labour, but there were also the days when little needed to be done or the weather did not allow any work to be done. There would be money earned by some employed in various process of cloth-making in the township, but how many is not known and depended on the current demand for cloth. It is probable that an income of no more than £2 a year was not unusual.

The tenants named at these courts were from families who had held tenancies in Mirfield for many generations. Leigh (Lee), Northorpe, Fournes and Bywater (Water or by the Water) were some of the oldest families and all had substantial holdings. The Northorpes had their hall and lands in Northorpe. a holding that was to be split and another house, the present Northorpe Hall was built. They were to be there until nearly the end of the seventeenth century. Lawrence of ye Leigh was probably at the house at the 'leigh' or 'green' (a piece of enclosed grassland) now Lee Green where there was an ancient oak tree by the house in Ismay's day. There were two men named John Leigh, one eventually at Hopton and John Leigh of Wellhouse in 1470 who also had land at Westroyd in Crossley. The Fournes family are less easily placed although they seem to eventually had part of the Northorpe land and the original Northorpe Hall, although by then they were living at South Kirby. Their tenants in Northorpe were the Stokkes, or Stocks. It is only by name that the 'by the waters', otherwise known as Bywater or Waters, are placed at Water Hall, the only large holding near the river which had been closer to the Earthorpe than it is now. It is interesting to note the mixture of surnames or descriptive names still used in 1485, some not yet fixed. as 'by the broke' (presumably the Townbrook) and 'by the water'.

The record from these manor courts presents a very partial picture of the township, the land and the freehold tenants. Families such as these were not only tenant landholders, but may have also been involved in some other business as were some of the Northorpe family who were merchants. Where there was other business, possibly in woollen cloth-making, land might also be leased to sub tenants. Some sons had an education that fitted them for a profession, or were apprenticed to merchants or craftsmen. One was Adam Fourneys of Mirfield, goldsmith in London in 1482, whose apprenticeship was probably expensive. The Mirfield family not only were lords of the manor, but had a long tradition as lawyers, probably educated at the Inns of Court in London. There was also Dr John Mirfield of Saint Bartholomews in London, who was well known for his writings on medicine and neurology. He died in 1407. It is not known whether he was born in Mirfield, but his family belonged here since no other place named Mirfield has been found to account for his name.

Towards the end of the fifteenth century more settled and prosperous times were returning, with the good harvests in the 1490s. The landscape was now beginning to resemble that described by parson Ismay at a much later time - a patchwork with small fields enclosed by quickthorn hedges and the large common fields that were dwindling in size. The distribution of land in the medieval fields, the holdings comprised of dispersed strips meant to give a fair share of land on the different soils and situations, had been slowly changing for a long time. Since the thirteenth century strips were sometimes being exchanged to give more conveniently worked blocks of land. Now some tenants were making further exchanges to gain enough land for a block of fields that could be enclose with hedges and ditches. The process by which this was achieved is well illustrated in a document recording an exchange of land made between John Northorpe and Thomas Stocks on the 21st March 1471. These lands were mostly in the south-east part of the township, the East Field or now Ravensthorpe. John Northorpe transferred to Thomas Stocks a block of 4 lands 'lying upon ye Impyard Flatts and next to other lands bounded and hedged and diked beneath Rood Rayne and adjoining enclosed parts of Impyard Flatts, being a part of the common field'. There were also lands hedged and ditched in the bottom Inge and other pieces mentioned were '3 lands bounded by New Dike head and in Colpittflatt'. There was a block of 4 lands in Shortweed and half a rood on Calderbank and much more. All of these lands were adjacent to land already held by Thomas Stocks and in exchange John Northorpe took land adjacent to some that he also already had.

Some of the substantial timber-framed houses of the more prosperous tenants were probably being enlarged with a cross wing that had upper storey chambers. Always the largest, and centrally placed near the church, was the Castle Hall, soon to be refurbished by Thomas Beaumont in 1522. Another major house was the Over Hall at the head of Towngate. There was the ancient tenement at Lee Green with its oak tree, an ancient and enormous tree still there in Ismays day, and the house belonging to the Wateroyd. There was the Wellhouse where John Lee lived; the initials 'R L' and a hammer on the stone doorway possibly a Richard Lee, a mason who may have stone clad the house in 1575. By then it was Gilbert Holdsworth's house as recorded on the date stone. There were two substantial houses at Northorpe, the Hall and the adjacent farm that became the new Hall .and beyond that hamlet the Fieldhouse at the edge of the Overfield, and later known as Primrose Farm. There was Robert Hopton's house, the later Blake Hall, and the old Parsonage with its tithe barn, the Earthorpe or Water Hall that overlooked the river and another farmhouse at the Earthorpe where the Black Bull now stands. At the far west side of the great moor was the old house, later to be called Yew Tree, and probably others not identified. Some of these houses almost certainly belonged to men who were involved in making cloth. There were also the small, low cottages with their heavy overhanging thatch; some in the Town, the Northorpe and the Earthorpe. None of the tenants of these can be identified and they have long since disappeared.

In addition, there were the barns and other farm buildings attached to the houses, some probably small workshops, some for cloth-making. There were also the two mills along the river, the corn mill and fulling mill at Westmills occupied in 1470 by John Gledhill and the corn mill and fulling mill below the Earthorpe later known as Ledgard mill. There was almost certainly a tannery, and had been since William the Tanner's time in 1202, and would be until much more recent times. There was always a demand for leather and the last of the Northorpes sold the Upper Hall to John Oates who was a tanner.

Sir William Mirfield's court had been held early in the year 1485, and in August of that year the battle of Bosworth brought the first Tudor king, Henry VII, to the throne. It is a date sometimes given as the end of the medieval period of English history and the beginning of modern times. There are however no clean breaks, neither in 1485 or 1500, the approximate end date for the history covered in this book. Manor courts continued to be held and well into the seventeenth century these were to deal with much the same business as that recorded for Williiam Mirfield's court in 1485. Land was still being cultivated in the common fields until gradual enclosure left the last few remaining strips in Shillbank Field. These were enclosed along with the great open space of Mirfield moor and the small pieces of common land by an Act in Parliament in 1798. The manors passed into other hands but eventually the Manor of Castle and the de Mirfield manor were brought together in the mid seventeenth century. Since that time the Saviles of Thornhill have been lords of the manor of Mirfield.

The once important families were to gradually disappear and by the end of the seventeenth century Northorpes were no longer at Northorpe after at least 500 years. The Bywaters of Earthorpe were gone by the sixteenth century and the Fourness not long after. The rectory remained in the hands of the prioress and Convent at Kirklees until the Dissolution of the Monasteries in 1539, and from that time there were to be lay rectors. The church continued as the centre of the community although with the changes in religious thought and practice which followed the Reformation the medieval building underwent some transformation. Probably in the seventeenth century much of the medieval glass disappeared when larger windows were put in place and galleries were then built, but much of the ancient fabric was still in place until the early nineteenth century. The landscape of medieval Mirfield was still recognisable when the Reverend Joseph Ismay walked around the parish and made his notes on what he saw and remarkably, despite all the overbuilding, traces of it can still be found today.

CHAPTER FOURTEEN

Epilogue
A Nun's Tale

Unexpected stories sometimes result from the coming together of small pieces of information and that concerning the last prioress of Kirklees is one. Thomas Stocks, the same whose exchange of land was recorded in 1471, died sometime before October 1508 and before his son and heir, Adam, had come of age and could take possession. Adam became the ward of their manorial lord, Sir William Mirfield, who would take the profits of his land and could also arrange a marriage for him. On the 22nd of October 1508, when Adam was nineteen years of age, an agreement made between Sir William Mirfield and Robert Kippax, vicar of Mirfield, that 'Adam Stocks should marry Janet Kippax, daughter of Thomas Kippax, if she was willing and agree'. The bride, either the sister or niece of the vicar, also seems to have been nineteen years old. The marriage was to take place before the next Christmas and an estate valued at 20s per annum was to be made for Adam out of the lands of the late Thomas Stocks and a settlement of £20 was to be made by Robert Kippax. As the pair should not live together until Adam was of age the income from the lands would be used for their maintainance. Sir William was to have 'the holding and keeping of the said Adam and find him in mete and drink and chamber and other more during his nonage and to have yearly 6s 8d from the said lands and tenements … towards the keeping of the said Adam during all his said nonage and like that the said vicar shall have the keeping of the said Janet from the same feoffement (lands) that is to say 13s 4d yearly towards her finding during the nonage of the said Adam'.

Adam had come of age in 1510 when 'Adam, son and heir of Thomas Stocks, late of Mirfield, and Johan, daughter of Thomas Kippax, were granted his lands'. By 1517 Adam was dead and his sister Margaret had married Robert Fourness. There appears to have been some sort of dispute because an agreement was made between Janet and her sister-in-law 'concerning the right and title to lands in Mirfield'. Margaret was named as Adam's heir. There are no other details. Presumably there were no children from the marriage between Adam and Janet and the widowed Janet is not mentioned again until much later.

In 1539, the king's commissioners for the closure of the monastic houses arrived at Kirklees to receive the surrender of the nunnery into the king's hands. The prioress, now Joan Kippax, was to make the surrender. As was usual at that time Janet or Johan Kippax, the name varies, had retained her own name after her marriage to Adam Stocks, and as sometimes happened with widows had entered the nunnery at Kirklees. She was to remain there for twenty or so years becoming prioress two years before the surrender. Kirklees was a small nunnery where local families, the Hetons, Hoptons, Mirfields and others of the better off had placed daughters in the past. Not a few lacked any vocation for the religious life and, being sent there, their behaviour had sometimes brought the nunnery into disrepute.

The closure had no doubt been anticipated at Kirklees and plans were made for the future. For Janet Kippax this was to return to Northorpe. The Stocks seem to have been tenants of the Fourness family and probably the old Northorpe Hall which would now belong to her sister in law, Margaret Furness. Ismay records the tradition that this was the houses where the nuns had lived. and the evidence of family connection and their ownership of the house makes it likely. Five nuns there formed a small community, something that is known from elsewhere, possibly with a way of life resembling in some ways that they had known for years. Four of them were elderly women by the perception of the times. As well as Janet Kippax, who was fifty years old, there was Isabel Hopton, now aged fifty, Agnes Brook, also fifty, and Isabel Rhodes aged forty, all women from local families. The youngest was Isabel Saltenstall aged twenty four. All had received pensions at the surrender. Janet Kippax died in February 1561, her burial being recorded in the parish register, something new then and only recently introduced. She was then probably about seventy two years of age, old by the standards of the times. Nothing further is known of the other four members of that small community; perhaps some had died before the new registers were made. By then, with the new Queen, Elizabeth, the new Protestant Church had been firmly established in law and religious communities were a thing of the past. It was the beginning of modern times and Janet the prioress was a woman of the medieval past. In the old church there was this inscription around an arch on the north side of the chancel:

'Dame Joan Keppas, late nun of Kirklees, buried February ye 5th day 1562'

Other than the name of the inn there is nothing to confirm the story of the three nuns who, it has been said, had a hostellery by the Nunbrook. An unlikely story, or does it have a grain of truth in it? In 1536 Kirklees had been reprieved from closure,

The Three Nuns c.1900.

one condition being that it would continue to provide 'both hospitality and other good works'. For travellers taking the routes up the Calder and Colne valleys into Lancashire, the nunnery at Kirklees was the last religious house that might provide food and lodging.

The three nuns may have been Joan Levenhtorpe, aged sixty years, Katherine Grice who was twenty five, and perhaps Cecilia Topcliffe, a former prioress, who was at least sixty years old; she had probably resigned as prioress in 1537. They may have stayed together and lived in a house nearby. Did they maintain the old tradition and use another barn or outbuilding to provide hospitality for travellers? The first mention of the Three Nuns, so far found, was in 1733 (Mirfield Township Books) but when the old Three Nuns Inn was demolished in the 1930s it was reported that remains of a fourteenth century building were found.

Sources used

The Manuscripts of the Reverend Joseph Ismay

> Of great interest and value have been the manuscript notes and diaries of the Reverend Joseph Ismay, vicar of Mirfield from 1735 to 1778. Although being largely a window into Mirfield in the eighteenth century, there are descriptions of Mirfield Parish, it's landscape and natural resources and references to local history and antiquities. The collection of Ismay's notes is deposited with the Yorkshire Archaeological Society who have given the kind permission for quotations from them.

The Turner Manuscripts

> The antiquarian notes of William Turner of Hopton, farmer and attorney, are largely copies of material to be found in the Ismay notebooks some of which he updated to about 1819, adding his own comments. These also are deposited with the Yorkshire Archaeological Society.

Savile of Rufforth archive

> These include several fragments of fifteenth century court rolls and rentals and more complete court rolls from the late sixteenth century and are held at Nottingham County Archive Office

Savile Estate papers

> More recent papers now deposited at at Huddersfield Public Library.

Beaumont of Whitley archive

> For plan of Castle Hall estate 1720. at Huddersfield Public Library.

Armitage of Kirklees archive

This has a range of deeds starting in the thirteenth century, material relating to the Rectory of Mirfield and estate plans. These are deposited with Calderdale Archives at Halifax Public Library;

Of the books consulted many are from series published by the Yorkshire Archaeological Society.

Ordnance Survey Maps

The first edition of the 6 inches to one mile (1854) and the first edition of the 25 inches to one mile (1897) have been the most useful.

Other maps and plans

These have come from the archive collections named above. They are plans of the Beaumont Estate in Mirfield made in 1720 and the same estate (Armitage) 1793. The Enclosure map, the survey made of '.the Waste Grounds and Town Fields within the Manor of Mirfield' 1798, which preceded the Parliamentary Act for enclosing the same. The post enclosure map showing some of the newly created enclosures is the Armitage Sale Plan of 1810 and Henry Harling's Map of Mirfield Township commissioned in 1819. This last is only available as a photocopies of the original and there are inaccuracies in the labelling which seems to have been done at a later date.

Air photographs

Photographs from the collection of Historic England (formerly English Heritage) taken in 1948 and 1954 and now held in the National Monuments Record.
Photographs by Meridian Airmaps Limited taken in July 1969. These were taken at a greater altitude and so provide a general overview of the landscape before the more recent overbuilding.
Air photographs of specific areas of interest were taken by by P.S. Thornes and M.G.Brook in 1997.

Abbreviations used in the text

Ismay	The deposited papers of the Rev Joseph Ismay.
Turner	The notebooks of William Turner.
Savile	Savile Estate Archive, Huddersfield
Savile (Rufford)	Savile of Rufford Archive, Nottingham.
Beaumont	Beaumont of Whitley Archive, Huddersfield
Armitage	Armitage of Kirklees Archive, Halifax.
O.S.	Ordnance Survey Maps.
Harling	Henry Harling's map of Mirfield Township 1819.
Enclosure Map	The Waste Grounds and Town Fields in the Manor of Mirfield 1796.